Bridging the Rift: A Pacifist Vision for the Israel-Palestine Future

Bridging the Rift: A Pacifist Vision for the Israel-Palestine Future

Kayumba David

Published by Kayumba David, 2024.

BRIDGING THE RIFT: A PACIFIST VISION FOR THE ISRAEL-PALESTINE FUTURE

First edition. November 4, 2024.

Copyright © 2024 Kayumba David.

ISBN: 979-8227753199

Written by Kayumba David.

Also by Kayumba David

1
Grow a Backbone and Walk out of an Abusive Marriage

Thanks to Calvary: A Salvific Treatise on the Cross
The centuries old swindlers

Watch for more at www.zcews.org.

Dedication

To the people of Israel and Palestine, whose enduring hope and resilience inspire this vision of peace. This book is dedicated to every mother, father, child, elder, and young adult who has lived with the weight of this conflict but still dreams of a life unburdened by fear and hostility. May this book serve as a small light on the path toward a shared, harmonious future. May you find in these pages a vision that echoes your deepest longing for peace, a peace that honors both your history and your future, a peace that is not merely the end of conflict but the beginning of a new relationship, grounded in respect, humility, and love.

Kayumba David

Dedication

To the people of Israel and Palestine, whose enduring hope and resilience inspire this vision of peace. This book is dedicated to every mother, father, child, elder, and young adult who has lived with the weight of this conflict but still dreams of a life unburdened by fear and hostility. May this book serve as a small light on the path toward a shared, harmonious future. May you find in these pages a vision that echoes your deepest longing for peace, a peace that honors both your history and your future, a peace that is not merely the end of conflict but the beginning of a new relationship, grounded in respect, humility, and love.

Preface

The Israel-Palestine conflict has endured for more than a century, becoming one of the world's most complex and entrenched struggles. It is not simply a matter of politics or territory, but a deep intertwining of cultural, historical, and religious identities. These identities are sacred to both Israelis and Palestinians, forming an integral part of their sense of belonging and purpose. For both communities, the land carries stories and symbols that reach back generations. It is this shared reverence for the land that makes the conflict so profound and, paradoxically, holds the potential for healing.

This conflict has tested the limits of diplomacy, resilience, and human suffering. Families on both sides have known loss, displacement, and trauma; generations have grown up in a world marked by checkpoints, borders, and a pervasive sense of "us" versus "them." Yet, despite the enduring pain and hostilities, there is also an enduring hope for a better future. This hope, fragile yet resilient, is the seed from which peace can grow.

Throughout the years, many approaches have been attempted—treaties signed, accords negotiated, and peace processes championed—yet they have faltered in the face of distrust and historical grievances. For too long, solutions have been structured on a zero-sum paradigm, where one side's gain was perceived as the other's loss. Such approaches have served only to deepen the divisions, entrenching each community in its own narrative of righteousness and victimhood.

This book envisions a way forward through a unique confederation model—a path not dependent on dominance but on coexistence, not on division but on shared governance. This confederation is a structure that respects the autonomy and self-determination of each community while fostering cooperation on shared issues. It allows both Israel and Palestine to maintain their own governance, culture, and identity, yet provides a framework through which they can work together as neighbors, partners, and ultimately, as a shared community.

In a world that has seen enough of war and division, a new chapter of humility and hope is required. True peace, as pacifist theologian Stanley Hauerwas reminds us, is not merely the absence of conflict but the presence of justice, respect, and mutual understanding. Hauerwas writes, "The work of peace is nothing less than the work of worship." Peace is not a passive state but an active practice, a deliberate commitment to see and honor each other as human beings made in the image of God. It requires humility to set aside pride and past grievances, and it demands courage to extend a hand rather than a fist.

This vision for a confederation is grounded in a theological and ethical framework that calls for peace as an act of worship and an expression of faith. It invites both communities to move beyond the wounds of history and into a relationship built on the values of compassion, justice, and shared humanity. It asks us to replace the narrative of power with the language of humility and mutual service. It is, at its core, a call to love one's neighbor in the most challenging of circumstances, a love that seeks not to erase difference but to honor it, to see the other's dignity and humanity.

This confederation model is not a quick fix, nor is it an easy path. It will require time, patience, and profound willingness from both sides to engage in the difficult work of reconciliation. But it also offers a vision of hope—a possibility that, after years of division, Israelis and Palestinians can build a shared future where they live side by side, not as adversaries, but as neighbors and co-citizens. This is not merely a political proposition but a moral and spiritual commitment to honor the sacredness of life and the dignity of each community.

This book is offered with the prayer that it may inspire both Israelis and Palestinians to see the beauty of peace, the strength of humility, and the power of shared governance. For when all else fails—when bombs and muscles fail—humility is the majesty that honors both

God and humanity. This path may be challenging, but it is also deeply rewarding, for it aligns with the divine call to seek peace, pursue it, and make it a reality in this world.

Chapter 1

Historical Roots and the Current Deadlock

The roots of the Israel-Palestine conflict run deep, nourished by centuries of religious, political, and cultural significance in a region where history and identity are woven tightly into the very fabric of the land. To understand the current deadlock, one must look back to pivotal historical events that have shaped Israeli and Palestinian narratives, molding their respective senses of belonging, grievance, and hope. This chapter explores some of these defining moments, considering how they have contributed to collective memory, national identity, and the contentious land claims that persist today.

The Ottoman Empire's Decline and the Dawn of Modern Nationalism

The decline of the Ottoman Empire in the late 19th and early 20th centuries marked a transformative period for the region. Palestine, part of the Ottoman Empire for nearly four centuries, was a diverse society where Arabs, Jews, Christians, and others coexisted under a shared imperial structure. But as the Ottoman Empire weakened, new ideas about nationalism began to take hold. For Arabs, this period sparked a sense of Arab identity and independence from imperial rule, while the Zionist movement began to take shape among Jews, particularly in Europe, who envisioned a homeland where they could escape persecution.

The concept of nationalism, which was reshaping Europe and other parts of the world, added new dimensions to the identities of both Jews and Arabs. Jews from Europe started migrating to Palestine, motivated by a growing Zionist vision that aspired to establish a Jewish state. This movement was born from centuries of persecution in Europe, pogroms, and a deep longing for a homeland. Palestinians, who already identified with their Arab roots, viewed these developments with increasing concern, perceiving a threat to their own cultural and demographic integrity.

As Stanley Hauerwas emphasizes in *The Peaceable Kingdom,* understanding conflict requires seeing the narratives and experiences of the "other." Hauerwas states, "We must remember that the work of peace requires us to learn how to see each other." This context invites readers to understand not only the Jewish yearning for security and homeland but also the Palestinian fear of displacement and loss. The seeds of the Israel-Palestine conflict were planted in this period, as each group sought to claim the land as integral to their national identity.

The Balfour Declaration and British Mandate (1917-1947)

The British capture of Palestine from the Ottomans during World War I and the subsequent issuance of the Balfour Declaration in 1917 marked another key turning point. In this letter, the British government expressed support for the establishment of "a national home for the Jewish people" in Palestine, while also stating that "nothing shall be done which may prejudice the civil and religious rights of existing non-Jewish communities."

The ambiguity of the Balfour Declaration, along with the dual promises made by the British to both Arabs and Jews, led to growing tensions and violent confrontations. Palestinians felt that their aspirations for self-determination were being ignored, while Jews, particularly European immigrants escaping anti-Semitic violence, saw the declaration as a validation of their hopes for a secure homeland. This era saw growing resentment between the two communities as more Jews migrated to Palestine, leading to clashes over land, jobs, and political representation.

The British Mandate period became marked by a series of uprisings, as both communities increasingly sought sovereignty. The Palestinian revolts in the 1930s, often violently repressed by British forces, and the Jewish resistance movements later on, reveal the deepening sense of dispossession and frustration on both sides. Rashid Khalidi, in *The Hundred Years' War on Palestine*, describes this period as one of betrayal and missed opportunities for both communities. The struggle for autonomy during the British Mandate would solidify grievances that would carry forward into future decades.

The 1948 War and the Creation of Israel

The declaration of the State of Israel in 1948 and the subsequent Arab-Israeli war were defining moments that reshaped the region irrevocably. For Jews, this was a moment of triumph—a fulfillment of their dream for a homeland where they could live free from persecution. The horrors of the Holocaust had intensified the desire for a Jewish state, and the international community's support for Israel's creation reflected a global acknowledgment of Jewish suffering and resilience.

However, for Palestinians, the events of 1948—what they call the Nakba, or "catastrophe"—represented a devastating loss. Hundreds of thousands of Palestinians were displaced, many forced into refugee camps in neighboring Arab states, where they and their descendants would remain for generations. Entire villages were destroyed, families were separated, and the trauma of dispossession became etched into the Palestinian psyche. This tragedy, compounded by the world's seeming indifference, would become a core element of Palestinian identity, solidifying a sense of injustice and yearning for return.

Stanley Hauerwas's insights into the nature of peace and reconciliation are essential here. Peace, he asserts, is rooted not just in the resolution of conflict but in the ability to honor and understand the suffering of the other. The events of 1948 created not only political division but also a deep emotional rift, one that has often prevented meaningful dialogue. As Hauerwas reminds us, "To live as if we can avoid suffering, avoid the suffering of others, is to turn our backs on our deepest connections."

The 1967 Six-Day War and Occupation of the Palestinian Territories

The Six-Day War in 1967 further escalated the conflict, leading to the Israeli occupation of the West Bank, East Jerusalem, Gaza Strip, and the Golan Heights. For Israelis, the war and its aftermath signified both a military victory and a biblical fulfillment, with territories of historical and religious significance now under Israeli control. This event strengthened the belief among many Israelis that they had a right to these lands, deepening the ideological commitment to settlements and security measures.

For Palestinians, the 1967 war was another Naksa, or "setback," an event that intensified their feelings of dispossession and solidified the image of Israel as an occupying force. The occupation created new layers of oppression, from military checkpoints to restrictions on movement, all of which became daily reminders of powerlessness. It is in these experiences of occupation that the Palestinian narrative of resistance took shape, with generations growing up in a world where their freedom and dignity were curtailed.

The occupation further complicated the peace process, as settlements expanded and Israelis and Palestinians became physically entangled in contested areas. This expansion, coupled with cycles of violence, entrenched mutual distrust and fueled radical ideologies on both sides.

The Emotional and Symbolic Weight of the Land

This chapter invites readers to consider the emotional and symbolic weight that both Israelis and Palestinians attach to the land. For

Israelis, it is the fulfillment of a promise, a refuge from historical persecution, and a testament to resilience. For Palestinians, it is their ancestral home, the heart of their cultural and historical identity, and the scene of generational trauma. Each side's attachment to the land is profoundly sacred and is woven into their identities in ways that defy political compromise.

Stanley Hauerwas's work on peace and identity speaks to this challenge. He writes, "Identity is not something that can be negotiated away; it must be embraced and transformed." The land is not merely real estate but a testament to each community's sense of purpose and connection to its past. To understand the conflict, one must see the land not simply as a resource to be divided but as a shared heritage that reflects the identities of two people.

The Current Deadlock: An Outcome of Historical Trauma and Collective Memory

The Israeli-Palestinian conflict today is characterized by a seemingly unbreakable deadlock, a product of accumulated historical trauma and collective memory. Each side's identity is tied to a narrative of suffering, survival, and entitlement, which has led to a situation where compromise is perceived as a betrayal of heritage. Palestinian collective memory is marked by displacement and occupation, while Israeli memory is defined by survival and the need for security. These narratives, though distinct, have intertwined in ways that prevent either side from seeing the other as anything but a threat.

As Hauerwas notes, "True peace can only be built when we learn to see beyond ourselves and listen to the stories of others." This chapter calls upon readers to engage deeply with the histories of both Israelis and Palestinians, understanding the grievances and aspirations that drive them. It urges an awareness that these historical events are not just memories but living experiences that continue to shape lives, policies, and perceptions.

Conclusion

Chapter 1 concludes by emphasizing the importance of understanding these historical roots not merely as past events but as ongoing realities that define the present deadlock. If there is to be hope for a confederation model, it must begin with an honest acknowledgment of these histories and the emotional landscapes they have created. Only by learning to see each other's suffering, loss, and hope can Israelis and Palestinians begin to imagine a future where their histories coexist, rather than clash.

References

- **Hauerwas, S.** (1983). *The Peaceable Kingdom: A Primer in Christian Ethics.*
- **Khalidi, R.** (2020). *The Hundred Years' War on Palestine.*
- **Armstrong, K.** (1996). *Jerusalem: One City, Three Faiths.*
- **Said, E. W.** (1992). *The Question of Palestine.*
- **Pappé, I.** (2006). *The Ethnic Cleansing of Palestine.*

Chapter 2

The Case for Confederation

For decades, the two-state solution has dominated peace negotiations between Israelis and Palestinians. Proponents of the two-state solution argue that dividing the land into two separate, sovereign nations could satisfy each side's desire for self-determination and security. However, repeated attempts have faced countless setbacks, largely because the land itself, particularly Jerusalem, is deeply sacred to both communities. Each community's desire for exclusive control over certain territories has proven to be a major obstacle, preventing a practical and sustainable division of the land. Given the realities on the ground, a confederation model—where Israel and Palestine retain internal autonomy but share governance over shared resources and concerns—offers an alternative.

A confederation does not require a complete separation; rather, it allows both communities to coexist within a structure that fosters cooperation, dialogue, and mutual responsibility. In this model, Israel and Palestine would remain distinct political entities with their own governments, laws, and cultural practices, yet they would cooperate on shared issues through a central governing body. This approach recognizes the unique needs of both communities while fostering interdependence, respect, and shared purpose. As Stanley Hauerwas writes, "Peace requires a people who embody peace." For peace to flourish, it must be cultivated not only in political treaties but in the daily interactions and shared institutions that make up a society. This chapter examines historical examples of successful confederations, highlights the unique features that make confederation viable in Israel-Palestine, and explores the spiritual dimension of this shared governance model.

The Limitations of the Two-State Solution

The two-state solution, while theoretically appealing, has encountered significant challenges that underscore its limitations. The main difficulty is the geographical and cultural interconnectedness of Israelis and Palestinians. Israel and Palestine are not two neatly divided communities; they are intertwined in terms of geography, culture, and historical narratives. Jewish and Palestinian populations are spread across various parts of the region, with shared holy sites, interconnected economic activities, and overlapping familial ties. Dividing the land with a strict boundary line is impractical given this interwoven reality.

Additionally, the two-state solution has often led to an "us versus them" mentality, where each community perceives the other as an existential threat to its sovereignty and security. This approach has fueled mutual distrust and fear, deepening divisions and making negotiations more difficult. The repeated failure of the two-state solution has led to disillusionment among both Israelis and Palestinians, prompting a rethinking of alternatives that could foster peace through collaboration rather than separation.

Confederation as a Model of Shared Governance

A confederation model offers a structure where both Israelis and Palestinians retain political autonomy within their communities but share governance on issues of mutual interest. This approach does not require an artificial division of land but instead allows each side to manage its internal affairs while working together on issues like security, economy, natural resources, and infrastructure. It acknowledges the interconnectedness of the two peoples and seeks to transform potential sources of division into opportunities for cooperation.

In a confederation, a joint council or central governing body would be established, where representatives from both Israel and Palestine would make decisions on issues affecting the entire region. This governing body would manage essential shared resources, like water and energy, ensuring fair distribution and preventing competition over scarce resources. Additionally, it could oversee joint infrastructure projects, trade policies, and environmental protections that benefit both communities.

The confederation model would also allow for shared access to Jerusalem, a city sacred to both Jews, Muslims, and Christians. Rather than dividing the city, a confederation would allow it to serve as a capital for both communities, a symbol of shared heritage and coexistence. Jerusalem could be governed by a special administrative council, representing both Israelis and Palestinians, with international oversight to ensure fair access and protection for all religious sites.

Historical Precedents of Successful Confederations

History provides several examples of successful confederations that managed to balance autonomy with shared governance, fostering peace and cooperation in diverse societies. Examining these examples offers valuable insights into the potential of a confederation in Israel-Palestine.

The Swiss Confederation

Switzerland is often cited as a model of peaceful coexistence among diverse linguistic and cultural groups. With four official languages—German, French, Italian, and Romansh—Switzerland is home to communities with distinct cultural identities. However, rather than dividing along linguistic lines, Switzerland operates as a confederation, with a decentralized government that grants significant autonomy to its cantons (regional governments) while maintaining a central federal structure. The cantons are responsible for local governance, including education, healthcare, and law enforcement, while the central government manages national defense, foreign policy, and economic regulations.

The Swiss model demonstrates that diverse communities can coexist and thrive within a shared structure, as long as each group retains autonomy over its affairs and has a voice in central governance. This approach fosters a sense of unity and shared purpose, even amid cultural and linguistic differences. Adopting similar principles, Israel and Palestine could respect each other's unique identities while cooperating on shared issues, thereby fostering a collective sense of responsibility and solidarity.

The European Union

The European Union (EU) is another example of a successful confederation that enables diverse nations to work together for common goals. The EU operates as a unique political and economic union where each member state retains sovereignty while collaborating on issues such as trade, security, and environmental policies. The EU has facilitated peace and economic growth among countries that were once adversaries, transforming Europe from a continent of warring states into a region of cooperation and stability.

The EU's success lies in its balance of autonomy and unity. Member states participate in a shared governance system but retain significant control over their domestic affairs. This model has allowed former enemies, like France and Germany, to build a peaceful and prosperous future together, using shared institutions to manage disagreements and build trust over time. Similarly, a confederation in Israel-Palestine could create channels for cooperation and conflict resolution, reducing hostilities through shared goals and mutual respect.

Confederation as a Spiritual Practice of Community-Building

The confederation model is not merely a political arrangement; it is also a spiritual practice that reflects core values of humility, respect, and interconnectedness. Stanley Hauerwas, in his book *War and the American Difference*, writes that "Peace requires a people who embody peace." This means that peace cannot simply be negotiated or enforced; it must be lived out through relationships, actions, and structures that reflect the values of coexistence and empathy.

A confederation model asks Israelis and Palestinians to reimagine their relationship not as adversaries competing for territory but as neighbors and partners who share the land. This vision requires a transformation in mindset—a shift from seeing each other as threats to recognizing each other as part of a shared community. Hauerwas's concept of peace as a "form of worship" suggests that working towards peace is an expression of faith and reverence for humanity, a commitment to honor each other's dignity and the sacredness of life.

The confederation model requires both communities to embrace mutual dependence, a challenging but spiritually enriching practice. By working together on issues of shared concern, such as water distribution, environmental protection, and public health, Israelis and Palestinians can build relationships based on trust and shared purpose. This approach aligns with spiritual principles found in both Jewish and Islamic teachings, which emphasize the importance of compassion, justice, and the recognition of our common humanity.

Overcoming Challenges and Building Trust

One of the primary challenges of a confederation model is overcoming the deep-seated mistrust between Israelis and Palestinians. Years of conflict have left scars on both sides, and building trust will require time, patience, and dedicated efforts. Establishing a confederal structure will not erase the history of violence or the pain of past grievances, but it can create opportunities for healing through shared responsibility.

Building trust requires transparency, accountability, and a commitment to addressing each community's concerns. The confederation model must include safeguards to protect the rights and autonomy of both sides, ensuring that neither community feels dominated or marginalized. Regular dialogue, joint decision-making processes, and equitable resource distribution will be essential for building confidence in the confederation's fairness and effectiveness.

Furthermore, international support can play a crucial role in facilitating this transition. Just as the EU helped facilitate post-war reconciliation in Europe, international actors could provide mediation, resources, and oversight to support the Israel-Palestine confederation. Neutral third-party oversight could help to monitor agreements, mediate disputes, and ensure compliance, providing both communities with a sense of security and accountability.

Conclusion: Confederation as a Path to Lasting Peace

The confederation model offers a path to peace that acknowledges the interconnectedness of Israelis and Palestinians, their shared history, and their mutual dependence on the land. It allows each side to maintain its identity and autonomy while building structures that foster cooperation and understanding. By shifting the focus from separation to shared governance, a confederation can lay the groundwork for a more peaceful and harmonious future.

As Hauerwas writes, "The first task of the church is not to make the world more just but to make the world the world." In the context of Israel-Palestine, this means creating a world where both communities can live with dignity, security, and respect. The confederation model is not merely a political solution; it is a call to embrace the values of peace, compassion, and shared responsibility. It is a model that invites both Israelis and Palestinians to see each other not as enemies but as fellow human beings, equally deserving of justice, freedom, and a place to call home.

References

- **Benvenisti, M.** (2000). *Sacred Landscape: The Buried History of the Holy Land since 1948.*
- **Hauerwas, S.** (2010). *War and the American Difference: Theological Reflections on Violence and National Identity.*
- **Gordon, N.** (2008). *Israel's Occupation.*
- **Lustick, I.** (2002). *Unsettled States, Disputed Lands: Britain and Ireland, France and Algeria, Israel and the West Bank-Gaza.*
- **Agha, H. & Khalidi, A.** (2005). *Track-II Diplomacy and the Israel-Palestine Conflict: The Swiss Initiative.*

Chapter 3

Governing Structures and Autonomy

In a confederation model, the governing structure for Israel and Palestine balances autonomy with cooperation, allowing each side to govern independently while participating in a shared federal council to address areas of common interest. This framework enables both communities to retain cultural and political integrity while fostering mutual dependency in critical areas like trade, immigration, environmental protection, and infrastructure. It seeks to provide a blueprint for coexistence in a region where the current structure has failed to bring lasting peace and stability.

This model requires a careful distribution of power to maintain each community's sense of sovereignty. Israel and Palestine would retain independent governments responsible for domestic issues such as education, healthcare, and law enforcement within their respective territories. Each government would operate within its own legal and political framework, respecting the unique cultural, religious, and social values of its population. However, a central confederal council composed of representatives from both sides would oversee issues that transcend borders and require joint management. This council would operate as a forum where representatives deliberate on matters affecting both nations and make decisions through consensus-building processes.

Stanley Hauerwas writes in *With the Grain of the Universe*, "The first task of the church is not to make the world more just but to make the world the world." Applied here, this philosophy calls for a model of governance that allows both communities to exist authentically within a shared space, without the need for one to dominate or assimilate the other. In this vision, Israel and Palestine are not adversaries vying for control but neighbors cooperating within a shared framework that honors their individuality and collective responsibilities.

Maintaining Autonomy: Independent Governments for Distinct Needs

Under this model, Israel and Palestine each retain their respective governments to address internal matters unique to their populations. This autonomy is crucial for ensuring that both communities feel their cultural and political identities are preserved and respected. Each government would operate independently in areas like education, healthcare, social welfare, and local law enforcement, maintaining full control over policies that shape daily life within its territory.

For Palestinians, this autonomy means the ability to create policies that reflect their national aspirations, culture, and language, and to exercise self-governance without interference. For Israelis, it allows for the continuation of existing structures and policies that align with their own national identity and security needs. By allowing each side to manage internal affairs independently, this model minimizes friction over domestic governance while promoting a sense of ownership and responsibility.

Autonomy also fosters accountability, as each government remains answerable to its own citizens rather than a central authority. This arrangement recognizes that the lived experiences and priorities of Israelis and Palestinians are distinct and that both communities need space to express their identities within a framework that respects their sovereignty.

Shared Federal Council: Addressing Mutually Critical Issues

The shared federal council is the cornerstone of the confederation model. This council would consist of representatives from both Israel and Palestine, tasked with addressing issues that impact the entire region and require joint oversight. By focusing on shared concerns, the council functions as a space for dialogue, negotiation, and problem-solving, where each side's voice carries equal weight.

Trade and Economic Collaboration

One of the primary functions of the federal council would be to manage trade policies and economic partnerships. Given the close proximity of the two communities, their economic health is inherently intertwined. The council would establish common trade regulations, manage customs at shared borders, and work toward economic initiatives that benefit both populations. By building an integrated economic framework, this model aims to create economic interdependence, making conflict less likely and collaboration more beneficial.

Economic cooperation could also extend to joint ventures in technology, tourism, and agriculture, sectors in which both communities could contribute unique strengths. Such partnerships would not only drive economic growth but also create opportunities for Israelis and Palestinians to work side by side, building relationships that transcend political divides. This collaborative approach, grounded in mutual benefit, can foster trust and demonstrate the advantages of interdependence over isolation.

Immigration and Freedom of Movement

Immigration and freedom of movement are sensitive issues, given the history of conflict and security concerns. The federal council would create policies to regulate movement between Israel and Palestine, allowing residents to cross borders for work, education, and family connections while maintaining necessary security protocols.

To address security concerns, the council could establish a joint immigration authority that manages border controls with oversight from both governments. This authority would handle visa and residency issues, ensuring fair and secure movement across borders. Freedom of movement policies would benefit both communities economically and socially, fostering a sense of openness and shared opportunity.

Environmental Regulation and Resource Management

Environmental issues, such as water resources, air quality, and land conservation, are crucial for both Israel and Palestine and are impossible to manage in isolation. The federal council would oversee these issues, creating policies that ensure sustainable and equitable resource use. Given the scarcity of resources like water in the region, collaboration is essential to prevent competition from turning into conflict.

Joint environmental initiatives, including water management, renewable energy projects, and pollution control, could be established through the council. For example, the Jordan River, a vital water source for both communities, requires careful management to avoid depletion and pollution. By approaching environmental issues collaboratively, Israelis and Palestinians can work toward a sustainable future that serves the interests of both sides.

Infrastructure Development and Public Services

Infrastructure is another area that would benefit from joint oversight. Roads, public transportation, energy grids, and waste management systems often cross borders and require coordination. The council would coordinate on infrastructure projects that connect both regions, facilitating movement and accessibility while avoiding duplication of resources.

Shared infrastructure could extend to public services like healthcare, emergency response, and disaster relief. Collaborative healthcare facilities, especially in border regions, could serve populations from both communities, fostering positive interactions and improving access to quality care. Likewise, a coordinated emergency response system could address natural disasters or public health crises, ensuring that resources are distributed equitably in times of need.

Ensuring Equitable Representation in the Federal Council

For this council to function effectively, it must operate on principles of equity and mutual respect. Representation in the council would be equal, with each side holding an equal number of seats or votes, regardless of population size. This structure is critical to preventing any one side from dominating decision-making processes and to ensuring that both communities feel that their interests are fairly represented.

The decision-making process within the council could be based on consensus or a supermajority, requiring a higher threshold for decisions to be approved. This model encourages dialogue and compromise, as representatives from both sides must collaborate to reach solutions that are acceptable to both communities. Such a structure ensures that issues of common interest are resolved through dialogue and negotiation rather than imposed by one side on the other.

Building Trust and Accountability

One of the challenges of any shared governance model is building trust between parties who have historically been in conflict. To promote transparency and accountability, the federal council could include an independent oversight body, composed of representatives from neutral international organizations, to monitor compliance with agreements and ensure fair implementation. This oversight would reassure both sides that the council operates fairly and that decisions are implemented as intended.

Regular public reports on the council's activities, decisions, and progress could further enhance transparency and build trust within both communities. Public engagement in council decisions—through consultations, referendums, or public hearings—would provide Israelis and Palestinians with a sense of ownership over the council's work and promote accountability.

Governing Structures as a Reflection of Ethical and Spiritual Values

The confederation model proposed here is not merely a pragmatic solution; it is also a reflection of the ethical and spiritual values that can sustain a just and peaceful society. Stanley Hauerwas's insight, "The first task of the church is not to make the world more just but to make the world the world," resonates deeply in this context. Here, "the world" represents a society where Israelis and Palestinians coexist in mutual respect, acknowledging each other's humanity and right to self-determination.

Hauerwas's philosophy emphasizes that the structures we create to govern ourselves should reflect our highest values and aspirations. In this confederation, the federal council becomes more than just an administrative body—it is an embodiment of a shared commitment to peace, justice, and cooperation. Each decision made within this council, each policy debated, is an opportunity to practice the values of empathy, respect, and mutual care.

In a region where identities are often seen as exclusive or adversarial, this model encourages Israelis and Palestinians to see themselves as interdependent parts of a greater whole. Through their participation in a shared governance structure, both communities have the opportunity to practice reconciliation and to build a society that values not just tolerance but genuine respect and understanding.

Conclusion: A New Vision for Governance in a Shared Land

The governing structure proposed in this chapter balances the need for autonomy with the benefits of collaboration, offering a model that allows Israelis and Palestinians to govern their own affairs while engaging in a shared federal council for issues that require collective management. This model does not ask either side to sacrifice their identity or sovereignty but invites them to see each other as partners in building a peaceful future.

By creating a framework where both communities can exercise autonomy while working together on shared concerns, the confederation model represents a transformative vision for Israel and Palestine—a vision that honors their individual histories and aspirations while fostering a shared commitment to peace and prosperity. This approach moves beyond the adversarial politics of division and toward a collaborative ethos that reflects the ethical and spiritual principles necessary for true peace.

References

- **Hauerwas, S.** (2001). *With the Grain of the Universe: The Church's Witness and Natural Theology.*
- **Cohen, H.** (2010). *The Rise and Fall of Arab Jerusalem: Palestinian Politics and the City since 1967.*
- **Bishara, A.** (2013). *Back Stories: U.S. News Production and Palestinian Politics.*

Chapter 4

Jerusalem: The Heart of Two Nations

Jerusalem stands at the heart of the Israeli-Palestinian conflict, a city that is both a source of division and a symbol of hope. Sacred to Jews, Christians, and Muslims alike, Jerusalem has been a spiritual and cultural beacon for millennia. It is the site of some of the world's most revered religious landmarks: the Western Wall, the Church of the Holy Sepulchre, the Al-Aqsa Mosque, and the Dome of the Rock. Yet, because of its significance to multiple religious and national identities, it has also been a focal point of political tensions, power struggles, and violence.

In this chapter, Jerusalem is proposed as a jointly governed international city—a place that reflects both the deep historical roots and the aspirations for peaceful coexistence. This shared administration model would treat Jerusalem not as a trophy to be claimed but as a sacred trust to be jointly honored and preserved. Drawing on examples such as Vatican City and Brussels, the chapter explores how cities with complex histories and overlapping identities have achieved stability and cooperation through shared governance. In this vision, Jerusalem can become a unique, globally recognized model for peace, demonstrating that diversity need not lead to division, and that mutual respect can replace control.

Stanley Hauerwas's statement, "The church is called to be a political alternative, not a partner in violence," resonates powerfully in this context. Here, Hauerwas challenges communities to embody a vision of peace that is radical and transformative. Just as the church can be a force for nonviolence, Jerusalem, governed as an international city, can become a political and spiritual symbol of unity, nonviolence, and coexistence. This chapter offers a detailed plan for this vision of

Jerusalem, rooted in historical precedent, spiritual significance, and pragmatic governance.

The Shared Governance Model: Learning from Historical Precedents

The proposal for Jerusalem as an international city is not without precedent. History offers several examples of cities with complex identities that have managed to coexist through shared governance arrangements.

Vatican City: A Religious and Political Hub

Vatican City, a city-state within Rome, serves as a powerful example of a location that holds unique religious significance for one community while existing within a broader political structure. Established as an independent sovereign entity within Italy through the Lateran Treaty of 1929, Vatican City is governed by the Holy See, serving as the administrative and spiritual center of the Catholic Church. This model respects Vatican City's unique role as a spiritual center while maintaining diplomatic and cooperative relations with the Italian state.

Applying this approach to Jerusalem would mean recognizing the city as an administrative and spiritual hub for multiple religions, while retaining a shared governance model. This structure could allow Jewish, Christian, and Muslim authorities to manage their respective sacred sites autonomously while working together on citywide policies through a central governing council.

Brussels: A Model of Multilingual and Multicultural Governance

Brussels, the capital of Belgium and the European Union, offers another relevant example. With both French-speaking and Dutch-speaking communities, Brussels operates as a bilingual city under a unique administrative arrangement that respects the linguistic and cultural identities of each group. It has a shared governance structure that ensures representation for both communities in local government, with policies crafted to address the needs and rights of all residents.

Like Brussels, Jerusalem is a city where multiple identities coexist. Establishing a governance model that reflects the multicultural, multilingual nature of the city would allow it to become a shared space where Israelis and Palestinians feel equally represented and respected. In this model, Jerusalem's administration could reflect the diversity of its population, with councils and committees formed to address the unique needs of each community. Such a structure could create a framework of cooperation and mutual respect, preventing any single group from exerting exclusive control over the city.

Governing Jerusalem: The Structure of a Joint Administrative Council

To achieve shared governance, Jerusalem could be administered by a joint council composed of representatives from both Israel and Palestine, as well as international observers or mediators to ensure transparency and fairness. This council would oversee key aspects of the city's administration, including zoning, infrastructure, public services, and the protection of holy sites.

Representation and Decision-Making

For the joint council to work, it must operate on principles of equity, ensuring that all communities have an equal voice in decisions affecting the city. Representatives from both the Israeli and Palestinian governments, as well as leaders from Jewish, Muslim, and Christian religious authorities, would have seats on the council. Additionally, international observers, possibly from neutral organizations like the

United Nations or the European Union, could act as mediators to facilitate dialogue and address any conflicts that may arise.

Decision-making within the council could follow a consensus model, or require a supermajority to pass significant policies. This would encourage deliberation and compromise, ensuring that decisions reflect the perspectives of all communities. A consensus-based approach would prevent any single group from dominating the council, while fostering an environment of respect and cooperation.

Protection and Management of Sacred Sites

One of the most sensitive aspects of Jerusalem's governance is the protection of its holy sites. Each religious community would have full authority over its respective sacred sites, with the joint council ensuring access and protection for all. This approach respects the sanctity of each community's traditions while preventing restrictions or discrimination.

To further safeguard the holy sites, an independent body composed of representatives from each religious group could be established to oversee maintenance, preservation, and security. This body would work in collaboration with the council to ensure that these sites remain places of worship, free from political interference or manipulation. The council would also ensure open access to all pilgrims, fostering a spirit of reverence and shared responsibility.

Public Services and Infrastructure Development

The joint council would also be responsible for overseeing public services and infrastructure projects in Jerusalem. This includes managing utilities, transportation, healthcare, education, and housing, ensuring equitable distribution across all neighborhoods. Public services would be provided without discrimination, treating all residents of Jerusalem as equal members of the community, regardless of ethnicity, nationality, or religion.

A joint police force could be established to provide security within the city, with officers drawn from both Israeli and Palestinian backgrounds. This force would operate under the joint council's authority, fostering a sense of shared responsibility for maintaining public order and safety. Officers could undergo joint training to emphasize principles of impartiality and cultural sensitivity, ensuring that security is enforced in a manner that respects all communities.

Jerusalem as a Symbol of Nonviolence and Unity

In his work, *A Community of Character*, Stanley Hauerwas reminds us that "The church is called to be a political alternative, not a partner in violence." This statement is a powerful reminder that faith communities—and the places they call home—should embody principles of peace, compassion, and understanding. Jerusalem, as a holy city central to Judaism, Christianity, and Islam, has the unique potential to be a living symbol of these values.

The city's role as an international capital for multiple faiths can serve as a reminder of our shared humanity and our mutual responsibilities. A jointly governed Jerusalem could stand as a global example of reconciliation, showing that diverse communities can come together to create a city of peace. This approach reflects the values of nonviolence and respect for the other, values central to all three Abrahamic faiths, and offers a model for other conflict-ridden regions around the world.

Addressing Challenges and Building Trust

Establishing Jerusalem as an international city governed jointly by Israelis and Palestinians will not be without challenges. Years of conflict have eroded trust between the two communities, and the memory of violence is still fresh for many. To overcome this history and build trust, transparency and accountability are essential.

Building Community Trust through Transparency

The joint council would need to operate with complete transparency, providing regular public reports on decisions, spending, and policies. Public consultations and feedback sessions could allow residents of Jerusalem to express their views and participate in shaping the city's future. This participatory approach would empower local communities and create a sense of ownership over the city's administration.

International Support and Oversight

The involvement of international actors in Jerusalem's governance can play a crucial role in ensuring that both Israelis and Palestinians feel secure. Neutral third-party observers could mediate disputes and monitor compliance with agreements. Their presence would provide both sides with the reassurance that Jerusalem's governance is being managed fairly and that their rights are protected.

Conclusion: Jerusalem as a Global Model of Peaceful Coexistence

In this shared governance model, Jerusalem can move from being a contested territory to becoming a symbol of peace, unity, and shared spiritual heritage. By embracing its status as an international city governed by both Israelis and Palestinians, Jerusalem can embody the peaceful coexistence that both sides desire. This model aligns with Hauerwas's vision of a "political alternative" grounded in nonviolence and mutual respect, inviting the world to see Jerusalem not as a city divided but as a city united in diversity.

A jointly governed Jerusalem can serve as a model for other contested regions, illustrating that peaceful coexistence is possible when there is a commitment to shared responsibility, transparency, and respect for each community's heritage. It offers a vision of governance that transcends political boundaries and reflects the ethical and spiritual principles that are at the heart of Jerusalem's significance.

References

- **Hauerwas, S.** (1981). *A Community of Character: Toward a Constructive Christian Social Ethic.*
- **Armstrong, K.** (1996). *Jerusalem: One City, Three Faiths.*
- **Lustick, I.** (2002). *Unsettled States, Disputed Lands: Britain and Ireland, France and Algeria, Israel and the West Bank-Gaza.*
- **Lapidoth, R.** (1996). *Autonomy: Flexible Solutions to Ethnic Conflicts.*

Chapter 5

Freedom of Movement and Citizenship

One of the fundamental pillars of a successful Israel-Palestine confederation is the establishment of freedom of movement and dual citizenship options. These measures are not only practical for the daily lives of people within the region but also represent a profound shift towards mutual recognition, respect, and the dismantling of psychological barriers that have kept Israelis and Palestinians apart. By allowing individuals to move freely within the shared space of Israel-Palestine and providing the option of dual citizenship, this model seeks to break down walls—both literal and figurative—that have historically divided communities.

This chapter explores the transformative potential of open borders and dual citizenship within a confederation. It examines the impact of restrictive policies, such as checkpoints, barriers, and limited travel permits, which have created an environment of fear, suspicion, and isolation. By advocating for open borders, this chapter presents a vision of mutual exchange and interaction, fostering relationships across cultural and national divides.

The words of Mahatma Gandhi resonate deeply in this context: "An eye for an eye will only make the whole world blind." Gandhi's teachings remind us that revenge and isolation perpetuate cycles of suffering, while peace is built through openness, empathy, and shared experiences. True peace lies in building bridges, not walls, and in allowing people to move freely and share life. Through this lens, freedom of movement and dual citizenship are not just policies but are pathways to a deeper peace.

The Impact of Restrictive Policies on Communities

For decades, restrictive movement policies have controlled the daily lives of Palestinians and Israelis, especially within the West Bank and Gaza. Israeli checkpoints, separation walls, and permits have limited Palestinians' ability to travel freely within their own territory and into Israel. This system has profoundly affected the lives of Palestinians, restricting access to work, education, healthcare, and family connections. For Israelis, the fear of violence and security concerns has led to a dependency on barriers as a form of protection, yet these measures have also isolated them from potential friendships and partnerships on the other side.

Restrictive movement policies have eroded trust, making it difficult for Israelis and Palestinians to view each other as anything but distant "others." Generations have grown up without meaningful contact with the other community, each side shaped by narratives of fear and suspicion. Without the ability to travel freely, the perception of the "other" becomes defined by stereotypes, media portrayals, and the trauma of past conflicts, rather than by personal relationships or lived experiences.

The economic consequences of these restrictions are significant as well. For Palestinians, limited movement has curtailed access to employment opportunities, restricted markets for goods, and prevented full participation in the regional economy. This economic disparity fosters resentment and frustration, fueling a sense of disenfranchisement. Similarly, Israelis are isolated from the cultural and economic richness that open borders could offer, missing out on the potential benefits of a collaborative and integrated regional economy.

By allowing freedom of movement within the confederation, this model offers a solution that goes beyond economics, addressing the social and emotional isolation that restrictive policies have caused. Open borders would enable people to access educational and employment opportunities, visit family members, and foster friendships across communities. This approach invites Israelis and Palestinians to see each other as neighbors and partners, moving past the walls that have divided them.

Building Bridges Through Open Borders

In a confederation, open borders between Israel and Palestine would allow for the free movement of individuals and goods, creating a more integrated and dynamic environment. This approach would not mean the removal of all border controls; security protocols could still be in place to ensure safety. However, these measures would operate under a framework of cooperation rather than division.

Open borders can be a catalyst for mutual understanding, allowing individuals from each community to experience the daily lives, struggles, and joys of the other. Cultural exchanges, shared marketplaces, and collaborative projects would foster relationships that transcend political boundaries. Israelis and Palestinians would have the opportunity to share life experiences, celebrate each other's festivals, and visit sacred sites. These interactions could help reduce prejudice and counter the narrative of perpetual enmity.

Open borders would also facilitate interdependence, where both communities benefit economically, socially, and culturally from the ability to work, trade, and interact freely. The benefits of interdependence are evident in many regions worldwide where neighboring countries have chosen cooperation over division. For example, the European Union's Schengen Area has allowed for unrestricted movement between member states, leading to economic growth and cultural exchange. Though Israel and Palestine's history and context are unique, the core principle of interdependence remains relevant: peace flourishes when people can share space, work together, and see each other's humanity.

Dual Citizenship as a Pathway to Inclusion and Equity

Offering dual citizenship within the Israel-Palestine confederation represents a commitment to equality and mutual respect. Dual citizenship allows individuals to identify with both Israel and Palestine, bridging the gap between national identities and fostering a shared sense of belonging. This approach would enable citizens to live and work in either territory, giving them the freedom to choose where they feel most at home while ensuring they retain political rights and responsibilities in their primary nation.

Dual citizenship also holds the potential to dismantle exclusionary mindsets. By recognizing the right of individuals to be citizens of both states, this model challenges the idea of exclusive ownership over the land. It acknowledges that multiple identities and allegiances can coexist within a shared space. For Palestinian refugees and those with family ties in Israel, dual citizenship would mean the ability to return or visit ancestral homes without compromising their Palestinian identity. For Israelis, it would affirm their connection to the land as a shared heritage, accessible and open to all who seek to live in peace.

The option of dual citizenship creates a pathway toward greater equality, ensuring that both communities feel secure in their rights and respected in their identities. This concept of dual identity aligns with the values of openness and inclusivity central to Gandhi's philosophy, which emphasizes the importance of recognizing and honoring the dignity of all individuals, regardless of their background or beliefs.

The Role of Security in an Open Borders Framework

One of the primary concerns regarding open borders is security. Decades of conflict and violence have left both Israelis and Palestinians wary of each other, and any plan for open borders must address legitimate security concerns. In this model, a joint Israeli-Palestinian security force, overseen by a neutral federal body within the confederation, would be responsible for maintaining peace and monitoring movement across borders.

The security force would include personnel from both communities who have undergone joint training to emphasize impartiality, cooperation, and respect. This joint force would operate under protocols agreed upon by both governments, with a focus on minimizing disruptions while ensuring public safety. Advanced technology, intelligence-sharing, and transparent processes could help create a security system that prioritizes the protection of all citizens without restricting freedom of movement.

An independent oversight body, possibly with international representation, could monitor the security arrangement to ensure that the rights of all individuals are respected. This oversight would be essential for building trust, as both communities must feel confident that security measures are fair, transparent, and designed to protect—not control—them. By working together in a shared security framework, Israelis and Palestinians can move past the image of the "other" as a threat and embrace a collective responsibility for peace.

Economic and Social Benefits of Freedom of Movement

Freedom of movement can significantly enhance economic stability and growth for both Israelis and Palestinians. By allowing Palestinians to access job markets and educational opportunities within Israel, and vice versa, the region's economy can become more dynamic, with a wider range of skills and resources benefiting both communities. Businesses, entrepreneurs, and professionals would have access to new markets, fostering innovation and collaboration that drive economic development.

Shared markets, trade routes, and tourism initiatives would allow Israelis and Palestinians to benefit from each other's strengths. For example, tourism to Jerusalem and other historical sites could become a collaborative effort, with Israeli and Palestinian tour operators working together to provide enriching experiences that celebrate the region's cultural diversity. In this way, open borders would not only bring economic prosperity but also create a model of cooperation that extends beyond political agreements into the realm of daily life.

Socially, open borders would allow families separated by decades of conflict to reconnect and provide opportunities for cultural exchange, joint projects, and interfaith initiatives. Schools, universities, and cultural institutions could collaborate on programs that promote mutual understanding, providing a new generation with the opportunity to grow up seeing each other not as adversaries, but as fellow citizens. Freedom of movement, coupled with dual citizenship, fosters a society where peace and cooperation are woven into the fabric of daily interactions.

True Peace as Bridge-Building, Not Wall-Building

As Gandhi's teachings remind us, "An eye for an eye will only make the whole world blind." The pursuit of revenge and the construction of walls have only deepened the divide, preventing Israelis and Palestinians from seeing each other as human beings with shared hopes and dreams. True peace requires a commitment to building bridges instead of walls, allowing people to connect, share, and learn from one another.

By removing physical and psychological barriers, the confederation model offers a vision of a future where Israelis and Palestinians can live side by side, united by shared experiences rather than separated by fear. This freedom of movement does not mean erasing boundaries or identities; rather, it acknowledges that identities can coexist within a framework of mutual respect.

In a shared Israel-Palestine confederation, freedom of movement and dual citizenship represent a commitment to inclusion and equity. They are not merely logistical conveniences; they are profound acts of bridge-building that open the door to a new chapter in the history of the region—one in which neighbors become friends, collaborators, and citizens of a shared land.

Conclusion: Toward a Future of Openness and Understanding

Freedom of movement and dual citizenship are essential components of a sustainable peace in Israel-Palestine. They represent a commitment to unity and respect for individual identities, allowing people to move, work, and interact without restriction. By embracing these principles, the confederation model offers a path to reconciliation, economic prosperity, and mutual respect.

Open borders invite Israelis and Palestinians to imagine a life where they can travel freely, share in each other's joys, and work together toward common goals. Dual citizenship affirms that individuals can belong to both Israel and Palestine, embracing the richness of both cultures. Together, these measures lay the foundation for a society where diversity is celebrated, and peace is not just a possibility but a lived reality.

References

- **Gandhi, M.** (2008). *The Words of Gandhi.*
- **Halper, J.** (2008). *An Israeli in Palestine: Resisting Dispossession, Redeeming Israel.*
- **Bar-Tal, D.** (2013). *Intractable Conflicts: Socio-Psychological Foundations and Dynamics.*
- **Cohen, H.** (2010). *The Rise and Fall of Arab Jerusalem: Palestinian Politics and the City since 1967.*

Chapter 6

A Unified Approach to Security

Security has long been a primary concern for both Israelis and Palestinians, with each community perceiving the other as a potential threat to its safety, stability, and survival. Decades of violence, fear, and mistrust have fostered an arms race mentality in which each side views increased militarization as a means of self-preservation. However, this approach has proven unsustainable, leading only to further entrenchment of conflict and escalation of tensions. To build a peaceful and cooperative future within a confederation, it is essential to redefine security as a shared responsibility rather than a battleground.

A unified security approach in the Israel-Palestine confederation model envisions cooperation between Israeli and Palestinian security forces under the oversight of a neutral peacekeeping council. This council would include representatives from both communities as well as neutral international observers, whose presence would provide accountability and assurance of fairness. Drawing inspiration from other regions with successful cooperative security models, this chapter explores how these frameworks can be adapted for Israel and Palestine.

Stanley Hauerwas's words offer a profound reorientation of the security paradigm: "To be a Christian is to be a pacifist. To be a pacifist is to be a Christian." For Hauerwas, pacifism is not merely about avoiding violence; it is a way of life that embraces reconciliation, empathy, and communal care. Applying this philosophy to a unified security approach shifts the focus from militarization to a shared vision of public safety. In this context, security becomes a means of protecting the dignity and rights of all people, ensuring that Israelis and Palestinians can live without fear.

The Limits of the Arms Race Mentality

The traditional approach to security in Israel and Palestine has been dominated by a mentality of escalation, where each side increases its own military capabilities in response to perceived threats from the other. Israel, with one of the most advanced militaries in the world, has invested heavily in defense technology, border security, and intelligence. Palestinians, particularly in the West Bank and Gaza, often rely on localized armed groups for protection, with some factions engaging in resistance tactics that have heightened hostilities.

This arms race mentality has resulted in a security landscape where both sides feel trapped, constantly preparing for the next conflict instead of working toward de-escalation. Israel's military strength, while providing a sense of security, has also led to a state of perpetual readiness, and the occupation has deepened Palestinian resentment and resistance. Meanwhile, for Palestinians, the lack of a formalized security infrastructure contributes to a sense of vulnerability and frustration. This security competition only deepens divisions, as each community increasingly views the other not as a neighbor but as an adversary.

A confederation model offers an opportunity to break this cycle by creating a framework in which security is not a zero-sum game but a shared goal. A unified approach recognizes that the safety of one community is intrinsically linked to the safety of the other, encouraging both sides to see each other as partners in peace rather than potential threats.

Learning from Cooperative Security Models in Other Regions

Several regions around the world have adopted cooperative security models that emphasize collaboration, transparency, and trust-building between groups with historical animosities. These models provide valuable insights for an Israel-Palestine confederation, demonstrating that shared security is both achievable and sustainable when structured properly.

The European Union's Common Security and Defense Policy (CSDP)

The European Union's Common Security and Defense Policy (CSDP) offers a model of shared security among diverse member states. Within the CSDP framework, EU countries collaborate on peacekeeping missions, disaster response, and border security, sharing resources and expertise to address common threats. This approach allows for joint security initiatives without infringing on the sovereignty of each state, creating a system where member states work together to ensure the safety of all.

In Israel-Palestine, a similar structure could be established, where Israeli and Palestinian forces coordinate on border security, counter-terrorism, and emergency response. The confederation's security council would serve as a central body for decision-making, establishing protocols, and overseeing joint operations. Each community would retain its security forces but work in tandem on issues that affect both populations. This model emphasizes collaboration over competition, recognizing that threats to security in one area impact the entire region.

The Good Friday Agreement and Northern Ireland's Community Policing

The Good Friday Agreement in Northern Ireland marked a turning point in a region long divided by religious and political conflict. One of the significant achievements of the agreement was the establishment of community policing, a system where law enforcement became representative of and accountable to both Protestant and Catholic communities. By building a police force that reflected the diversity of the population, Northern Ireland created a security model that fostered trust, reduced tensions, and encouraged dialogue.

A similar approach could be adopted within the Israel-Palestine confederation. By creating a joint security force composed of both Israeli and Palestinian officers, the confederation could promote a sense of shared responsibility for public safety. Officers would undergo joint training, emphasizing impartiality, respect for human rights, and cultural sensitivity. This training would be essential for building a security force that is trusted by both communities and capable of addressing security concerns in a balanced manner.

Structure and Oversight of the Unified Security Council

The central body for overseeing security in the Israel-Palestine confederation would be the Unified Security Council. This council would consist of representatives from both Israeli and Palestinian governments, as well as neutral international observers. The role of the international observers would be to provide accountability and transparency, ensuring that security operations adhere to the principles of fairness, justice, and respect for human rights.

Composition and Decision-Making

The council's composition would be balanced, with equal representation from both sides to prevent any one community from dominating decision-making. Decisions within the council could require a supermajority, encouraging consensus-building and collaborative problem-solving. This structure would ensure that security policies are crafted with input from both Israelis and

Palestinians, addressing the unique needs and concerns of each community.

The council's responsibilities would include setting joint security protocols, overseeing border management, coordinating intelligence-sharing, and deploying joint security forces in areas where both communities are present. By establishing unified standards and protocols, the council would help build trust and create a cohesive security strategy that prioritizes the well-being of all citizens.

Joint Security Force and Community Engagement

One of the most transformative aspects of this model is the creation of a joint security force, composed of Israeli and Palestinian officers working together to maintain peace and security. This force would be deployed in areas where both communities live, such as Jerusalem, and in border regions where tensions are highest.

The joint force would not only symbolize the commitment of both sides to coexist peacefully but also serve as a practical measure to prevent unilateral actions that could reignite conflict. Officers would be trained to respond to crises without bias, focusing on de-escalation and conflict resolution. By working together in mixed units, officers would learn to see each other as partners rather than adversaries, fostering a sense of unity and shared purpose.

Additionally, the joint force could engage with local communities through regular meetings, feedback sessions, and educational programs. Community engagement would be essential for building trust and ensuring that security measures align with the needs and values of the people they serve. By involving the community in security processes, the confederation would create a more inclusive, transparent, and accountable security system.

Embracing a Vision of Public Safety Over Militarization

The confederation model's unified approach to security represents a shift from militarization to a vision of public safety. Rather than focusing on building stronger defenses, the model emphasizes creating an environment where both Israelis and Palestinians feel secure without relying on military force. This approach aligns with Hauerwas's pacifist philosophy, which suggests that true security is found not in the accumulation of arms but in the establishment of systems that foster trust, respect, and interdependence.

In practical terms, this vision of public safety would prioritize preventive measures, such as conflict resolution, education, and community-building initiatives, over punitive actions. By addressing the root causes of insecurity—such as poverty, unemployment, and lack of education—the unified security approach seeks to create a society where people are less likely to resort to violence. Public safety becomes a collaborative effort, with the understanding that the safety of one community enhances the safety of the other.

Building Trust Through Transparency and Accountability

Trust is the foundation of any successful security model, and building trust between Israelis and Palestinians will require transparency and accountability at every level. The presence of international observers within the Unified Security Council would serve as a neutralizing influence, ensuring that security operations are conducted fairly and without favoritism. Observers would report on council activities, monitor compliance with agreements, and provide an impartial perspective in cases of conflict.

Regular public reports on security measures, budgets, and decisions would also enhance transparency, giving citizens confidence that their safety is being managed with integrity. Community feedback channels, such as public forums or complaint hotlines, would allow residents to voice concerns and offer suggestions, fostering a sense of involvement and accountability.

Conclusion: A New Approach to Shared Security

A unified approach to security within the Israel-Palestine confederation represents a radical departure from the adversarial model that has dominated the region for so long. By replacing the arms race mentality with a shared vision of public safety, this model invites Israelis and Palestinians to see each other not as threats but as partners in the pursuit of peace. It embraces Hauerwas's call for a pacifist approach, where security is rooted in trust, cooperation, and mutual respect.

The unified security approach challenges both communities to redefine what it means to be safe. It proposes that true security cannot be achieved through isolation or domination but through a commitment to shared responsibility and communal care. In this vision, Israelis and Palestinians work together to protect each other's rights and lives, building a future where security is a common good rather than a source of division.

References

- **Hauerwas, S.** (2010). *War and the American Difference: Theological Reflections on Violence and National Identity.*
- **Bar-Tal, D.** (2013). *Intractable Conflicts: Socio-Psychological Foundations and Dynamics.*
- **Mitchell, C.** (2010). *The Structure of International Conflict.*
- **Cohen, H.** (2010). *The Rise and Fall of Arab Jerusalem: Palestinian Politics and the City since 1967.*

Chapter 7

Economic Collaboration and Prosperity

Economic interdependence is a cornerstone of a peaceful and sustainable Israel-Palestine confederation. While political solutions can lay the groundwork for peace, economic collaboration can transform peace from a temporary arrangement into a thriving, mutually beneficial reality. A successful confederation would require an integrated economy that benefits both Israelis and Palestinians, creating shared incentives for maintaining stability and fostering a sense of unity. This chapter explores how joint economic initiatives, revenue-sharing mechanisms, and policies to reduce poverty can build mutual prosperity and trust between the two communities.

Martin Luther King Jr. said, "True peace is not merely the absence of tension: it is the presence of justice." Economic justice, therefore, must be the foundation upon which this confederation rests. For too long, economic disparity has fueled resentment and frustration, deepening divides and breeding suspicion. The confederation model calls for a vision of economic justice where both Israelis and Palestinians can share in the fruits of the land, enjoy equal opportunities, and collaborate in joint ventures that enhance quality of life for all. This chapter examines practical ways to achieve economic justice through shared initiatives, and how a thriving economic partnership can cultivate stability, dignity, and peace.

The Current Economic Disparities and Challenges

Before exploring potential solutions, it is essential to understand the economic disparities between Israelis and Palestinians that have developed over decades. Israel boasts a highly developed economy, with advanced technology, healthcare, and infrastructure sectors. By contrast, the Palestinian economy, particularly in the West Bank and

Gaza, has been constrained by restrictions on movement, limited access to natural resources, and challenges stemming from political instability. The Palestinian economy is heavily dependent on international aid, and high unemployment rates, especially among young people, contribute to poverty and frustration.

These economic disparities are not merely numbers on a balance sheet; they are deeply felt realities that impact the daily lives of Palestinians. Lack of access to basic services, limited employment opportunities, and dependency on external aid have created a situation where economic insecurity fuels political grievances. For Israelis, the economic divide creates a society where peace is fragile, as economic hardship across the border can lead to resentment, instability, and potentially, conflict. Reducing economic inequality, therefore, is not only an ethical imperative but a strategic one, crucial for building a resilient and enduring peace.

Shared Economic Initiatives for Growth and Stability

A confederation model envisions a range of joint economic initiatives that would benefit both communities, creating interdependence and mutual incentives for cooperation. These initiatives could span multiple sectors, from agriculture and tourism to technology and infrastructure.

Joint Infrastructure Projects

Infrastructure is essential for a thriving economy, but infrastructure development requires significant investment and cooperation, particularly in areas like transportation, energy, and water management. The confederation's joint council could coordinate infrastructure projects that connect Israeli and Palestinian territories, creating efficient transportation networks, shared power grids, and water distribution systems.

For example, building a robust public transportation system connecting key cities in both Israel and Palestine could ease the movement of workers, students, and goods. A shared power grid and energy projects, especially in renewable energy, could reduce dependence on external sources and lower energy costs for both communities. Joint water management projects would be particularly valuable in the arid region, ensuring equitable access to this critical resource.

Collaborative Agricultural Ventures

Agriculture is another area with significant potential for collaboration. By creating joint agricultural ventures, Israelis and Palestinians could increase food security, boost exports, and foster sustainable land use. Palestinian farmers would gain access to advanced agricultural technology and markets within Israel, while Israeli agricultural companies would benefit from labor and land resources in Palestine. Collaborative farming initiatives could promote sustainable practices, such as water-efficient irrigation and climate-resilient crops, benefiting the environment and the economy.

These agricultural projects could be managed by cooperative enterprises owned by both Israeli and Palestinian stakeholders. Such enterprises would share profits, ensuring that both communities benefit. By working together to improve food security, increase exports, and boost rural economies, Israelis and Palestinians would create jobs and reduce poverty in rural areas, helping to foster economic equality.

Tourism and Cultural Exchange

Tourism is another industry with great potential for generating shared revenue and fostering cultural exchange. The rich historical and religious significance of the land attracts millions of visitors annually, yet much of the potential for tourism remains untapped due to political tensions and restrictions. A peaceful, cooperative confederation could create a framework where Israelis and Palestinians work together to develop and promote tourism.

Jointly managed tourism initiatives could ensure that revenues are fairly distributed between the two communities. Israelis and Palestinians could collaborate on the promotion of key historical, cultural, and religious sites, such as Jerusalem, Bethlehem, and Nazareth. Tour operators, hotels, and local businesses would benefit from increased tourism, providing jobs and economic opportunities across the region. Joint tourism would not only stimulate economic growth but also encourage cross-cultural understanding and mutual respect.

Revenue-Sharing Mechanisms for Equity and Fairness

For economic collaboration to be truly successful and equitable, it is essential to establish revenue-sharing mechanisms. Shared revenues would help address existing economic imbalances, allowing the benefits of joint ventures and natural resources to be distributed fairly.

Tax Revenue Sharing

In the confederation, a proportion of tax revenue collected from cross-border economic activities and joint ventures could be allocated to a shared fund. This fund would then be used to support infrastructure, education, and healthcare in both Israeli and Palestinian communities, with a focus on addressing economic disparities. This approach ensures that economic gains from shared projects benefit both sides, contributing to equality and fostering goodwill.

Shared Resource Revenue

Natural resources, such as water from the Jordan River or minerals from the Dead Sea, should be shared and managed equitably. A revenue-sharing agreement would ensure that any profits derived from natural resources are divided between Israel and Palestine, based on mutually agreed-upon percentages. This system would prevent disputes over resources and provide a stable source of revenue for both communities.

By promoting equitable distribution of resources, revenue-sharing mechanisms help mitigate economic inequalities, ensuring that both Israelis and Palestinians benefit from the wealth generated within the confederation. Such mechanisms reflect the principle of economic justice that Martin Luther King Jr. emphasized—a justice rooted in fairness, equity, and the recognition of mutual dependence.

Addressing Poverty and Unemployment Through Social Programs

Reducing poverty and unemployment is essential for building a stable, peaceful confederation. The confederation's joint council could create programs aimed at reducing unemployment, particularly among young people, and addressing the root causes of poverty. Such programs might include vocational training, micro-loans for small businesses, and job creation initiatives in high-demand sectors like technology, construction, and healthcare.

Vocational Training and Education Programs

Investing in education and vocational training programs tailored to the needs of both communities would empower young Israelis and Palestinians with skills to participate fully in the labor market. Joint educational institutions could focus on fields that are crucial for economic development, such as technology, engineering, and healthcare. By collaborating on education, the confederation can foster a generation of skilled workers equipped to meet the region's economic needs and create a foundation for innovation and economic growth.

Micro-loans and Support for Small Businesses

Small businesses are vital to local economies, particularly in rural and low-income areas. The confederation's economic council could establish a micro-loan program to support small business owners and entrepreneurs from both communities. Access to small loans would enable individuals to start or expand businesses, create jobs, and contribute to economic stability. By investing in small businesses, the confederation would stimulate grassroots economic growth and promote financial independence, particularly for vulnerable populations.

Job Creation in High-Demand Sectors

Focusing on high-demand sectors, such as information technology, renewable energy, and healthcare, the confederation could create job opportunities that benefit both communities. For instance, Israel's advanced tech industry could collaborate with Palestinian tech entrepreneurs to establish joint tech hubs. These hubs could become centers for innovation, attracting international investment and offering high-paying jobs to skilled workers from both sides.

Economic Justice as a Foundation for Peace

Economic justice lies at the heart of the confederation's vision for a peaceful, thriving society. As Martin Luther King Jr. noted, "True peace is not merely the absence of tension: it is the presence of justice." Economic justice, in this context, means addressing the disparities that have created feelings of resentment and disempowerment, ensuring that prosperity is shared rather than monopolized. By fostering economic equity, the confederation can lay the groundwork for genuine, lasting peace, where neither side feels marginalized or excluded.

Economic justice also means providing equal opportunities for individuals from both communities to pursue their aspirations, live with dignity, and build a secure future for their families. By ensuring that the benefits of economic collaboration are shared, the confederation strengthens the bond between Israelis and Palestinians, fostering a sense of shared destiny and mutual support.

Building Trust Through Economic Interdependence

Economic interdependence can be a powerful force for peace, as it creates mutual benefits and a shared interest in stability. When Israelis and Palestinians work together to build a prosperous economy, they become stakeholders in each other's success. This interdependence fosters a pragmatic alliance, encouraging both sides to maintain peace and resolve conflicts through dialogue rather than confrontation.

As Israelis and Palestinians experience the tangible benefits of cooperation, trust can gradually be built. Successful joint ventures and revenue-sharing initiatives create a new narrative—one where collaboration is seen not as a compromise but as a pathway to shared prosperity. Through economic interdependence, the confederation can transform former adversaries into partners in building a society where everyone has the opportunity to thrive.

Conclusion: Economic Prosperity as a Catalyst for Peace

Economic collaboration is not a panacea, but it is a crucial element of a successful Israel-Palestine confederation. By embracing shared initiatives, establishing revenue-sharing mechanisms, and addressing poverty and unemployment, the confederation can create a robust economy that benefits all. In this vision, economic prosperity is not only a goal but also a means of fostering unity, reducing tensions, and laying the groundwork for a peaceful and equitable future.

The pursuit of economic justice, as advocated by Martin Luther King Jr., offers a pathway to a society where dignity and equality are the norm. A thriving economy, built on shared prosperity, enables both Israelis and Palestinians to see each other as partners rather than adversaries. Economic collaboration, rooted in justice and interdependence, can become a catalyst for peace, ensuring that both communities enjoy the benefits of a prosperous and stable future.

References

- **King, M. L.** (1963). *Strength to Love.*
- **Pappe, I.** (2006). *The Ethnic Cleansing of Palestine.*
- **Roy, S.** (1995). *The Gaza Strip: The Political Economy of De-development.*
- **Hassassian, M.** (2002). *Palestinian Political Discourse and Realities in the West Bank and Gaza.*

Chapter 8

A Joint Legal System

For a confederation between Israel and Palestine to be effective and sustainable, it must be grounded in a robust and equitable legal framework. A joint legal system within this confederation must respect the distinct cultural, religious, and legal traditions of both Israelis and Palestinians while upholding universal principles of justice, equality, and human rights. This chapter explores the structure and function of a joint legal system that balances autonomy with shared governance. Such a framework could include joint courts, neutral arbitration mechanisms, and protective measures for minority rights, creating a legal landscape that fosters trust, transparency, and cooperation.

Stanley Hauerwas's words offer an ethical foundation for this endeavor: "The language of peace is learned through worship and practice." A legal system built on peace and justice embodies this philosophy, emphasizing the importance of ongoing, practiced cooperation and mutual respect. It provides a space where both communities can seek redress, resolve disputes, and protect their rights without fear or prejudice. By creating a joint legal system, the confederation would demonstrate that peace is not only a political arrangement but a lived experience, practiced daily through the fair and respectful treatment of all people.

Balancing Autonomy and Shared Legal Responsibility

In a confederation, the legal framework must balance each community's autonomy in governing internal matters with the need for a unified approach to issues that affect both communities. This dual system would allow Israel and Palestine to maintain their own legal structures for domestic issues while collaborating on a joint legal system to handle inter-community matters. This approach ensures that each community retains its unique identity and traditions, fostering respect for cultural differences within a shared political entity.

Autonomous Legal Systems for Domestic Matters

Within this model, each state would retain full autonomy over its internal legal matters. This autonomy would allow Israel and Palestine to govern areas such as family law, religious practices, education, and other aspects deeply tied to cultural and religious identity. For example, Israel could continue to operate under its existing legal framework, which combines secular and religious laws, while Palestine could govern domestic issues according to its legal principles. This arrangement preserves the distinctive legal traditions of each community, ensuring that both Israelis and Palestinians feel their cultural identities are respected and safeguarded.

A Shared Legal Framework for Joint Concerns

Alongside the autonomous legal systems, the confederation would establish a shared legal framework to handle issues affecting both communities. These issues could include cross-border trade, environmental regulations, human rights, and any disputes arising from joint initiatives. A joint legal system is essential for addressing conflicts that transcend borders and ensuring that the confederation operates smoothly and fairly. This framework would function as a unifying structure, promoting consistency in how shared matters are handled, while leaving space for each community's domestic autonomy.

Joint Courts and Arbitration Mechanisms

A fair and effective joint legal system requires institutions where both Israelis and Palestinians can seek justice without bias. Establishing joint courts and neutral arbitration mechanisms would ensure that inter-community disputes are resolved impartially, with respect for both parties' rights and interests.

Joint Courts

Joint courts would be established to handle cases involving individuals from both communities or issues related to the confederation's shared responsibilities. These courts could focus on areas such as property disputes, cross-border commerce, and human rights violations. Judges in these courts would be selected from both Israeli and Palestinian legal communities, ensuring a balanced perspective in decision-making. To foster trust, international legal experts or neutral observers could also be appointed to the bench, providing a layer of accountability and impartiality.

The joint courts would be guided by a legal code agreed upon by both communities, rooted in principles of justice, human rights, and non-discrimination. This code would be crafted to align with international human rights standards, providing protections for all individuals within the confederation. By creating a unified legal code for shared issues, the joint courts would help establish a culture of fairness and respect across both communities.

Neutral Arbitration Mechanisms

In addition to joint courts, the confederation could establish neutral arbitration panels to resolve disputes that may not require a formal court process. These arbitration panels would provide a faster, more flexible alternative for resolving minor disputes, such as contractual disagreements or resource allocation issues. Arbitration panels would include mediators from both communities, as well as international mediators to ensure impartiality.

Arbitration is particularly useful for conflicts that arise within joint initiatives, such as business partnerships, shared infrastructure projects, or environmental resource management. By offering a process that is efficient and accessible, arbitration can help prevent minor disputes from escalating into larger conflicts. It also fosters a culture of dialogue and compromise, encouraging Israelis and Palestinians to work through differences cooperatively.

Protecting Minority Rights

A key component of a successful joint legal system is the protection of minority rights. Given the history of conflict and mistrust, it is essential to ensure that all individuals—whether they belong to the Israeli or Palestinian community—feel secure and valued within the confederation. This includes protecting the rights of individuals who may find themselves as minorities within the larger framework, such as Palestinians living in Israel or Israelis residing in Palestinian territories.

Constitutional Protections for Minorities

The confederation's legal framework could include constitutional protections for minorities, guaranteeing their rights regardless of where they reside within the confederation. These protections would cover areas such as freedom of religion, freedom of expression, and equal access to education, healthcare, and employment opportunities. By enshrining these rights in the confederation's constitution, the legal system would ensure that minority communities are treated with respect and dignity.

Constitutional protections would be reinforced by mechanisms for accountability, such as an independent human rights commission. This commission could investigate complaints of discrimination or abuse, providing a platform for minorities to seek redress. Such institutions would not only protect individuals' rights but also signal the confederation's commitment to justice and equality.

Language and Cultural Rights

Language and cultural rights are essential components of minority protections in a multicultural confederation. Recognizing both Hebrew and Arabic as official languages would be a powerful step toward ensuring that all individuals feel included and respected. Public institutions, schools, and legal documents would be available in both languages, allowing everyone to access government services and the legal system in their native language.

Furthermore, cultural rights would allow each community to maintain its traditions and religious practices without interference. This recognition is essential for creating a confederation that respects the diversity of its citizens. By promoting inclusivity and honoring the unique heritage of each community, the confederation would foster a sense of belonging and unity.

Learning from International Examples of Joint Legal Systems

Other regions with complex histories of conflict and diversity have successfully implemented joint legal systems that balance autonomy with shared governance. These examples provide valuable lessons for an Israel-Palestine confederation.

The European Court of Human Rights

The European Court of Human Rights (ECHR) serves as a supranational legal body that oversees human rights issues among

European countries. Individuals from any member state can bring cases to the ECHR if they believe their rights have been violated. The ECHR's role in providing an impartial venue for human rights cases has been instrumental in promoting justice and protecting minority rights across Europe.

A similar body within the Israel-Palestine confederation could serve as an appeals court for human rights issues. This court could ensure that individuals have recourse if they feel that their rights have been infringed, providing a critical safeguard for justice. By offering an avenue for legal redress, such a court would also build trust, reinforcing the confederation's commitment to upholding human rights.

The Swiss Federal Tribunal

Switzerland's federal legal system is another example of effective governance in a multicultural context. Switzerland's cantons (regional divisions) retain significant autonomy over legal matters, yet they operate within a unified federal system. The Swiss Federal Tribunal serves as the country's highest court, overseeing matters that transcend cantonal boundaries while respecting the distinct identities of each canton.

In the Israel-Palestine confederation, a similar model could be adopted, where local legal systems retain autonomy while a central tribunal or joint court oversees confederation-wide issues. This approach would promote coherence in handling cross-border matters while respecting the diversity of each region's legal traditions. The Swiss example illustrates how a decentralized yet unified legal structure can create stability and harmony in a pluralistic society.

Building Trust Through Transparency and Accessibility

A joint legal system can only be effective if it is transparent, accessible, and trusted by all citizens. The confederation's legal institutions would need to ensure that individuals from both communities feel confident in their ability to access justice. This could be achieved through a range of initiatives:

Public Information Campaigns: To build trust in the joint legal system, the confederation could conduct public information campaigns to educate citizens on their rights and the legal resources available to them. This outreach could include multilingual materials, workshops, and community forums to ensure that everyone understands how to access legal services.

Legal Aid Programs: Legal aid programs would be essential to ensure that all individuals, regardless of income, can seek justice. These programs would provide financial support for individuals who need legal representation, ensuring that justice is accessible to everyone, not just those who can afford it.

Transparency and Accountability Mechanisms: Transparency measures, such as public reports on court activities, regular reviews of legal procedures, and independent oversight bodies, would foster accountability and confidence in the joint legal system. By demonstrating a commitment to fairness, the confederation would build trust and show that it values justice for all.

Conclusion: A Legal System as a Foundation for Lasting Peace

A joint legal system within the Israel-Palestine confederation is more than a set of institutions—it is a practice of mutual respect, justice, and peace. By creating a framework that respects cultural differences while protecting fundamental rights, the confederation lays the groundwork for a peaceful coexistence where both communities feel secure, respected, and valued.

As Stanley Hauerwas reminds us, "The language of peace is learned through worship and practice." In this context, a legal system built on principles of peace and justice embodies this learning, fostering a culture where cooperation becomes a daily reality. Through joint courts, neutral arbitration, and protections for minority rights, the confederation's legal framework would offer a path toward justice and reconciliation, allowing Israelis and Palestinians to build a future grounded in fairness, trust, and mutual care.

References

- **Hauerwas, S.** (1981). *A Community of Character: Toward a Constructive Christian Social Ethic.*
- **Kattan, V.** (2009). *The Palestine Question in International Law.*
- **Crawford, J.** (2006). *The Creation of States in International Law.*
- **Shlaim, A.** (2009). *Israel and Palestine: Reappraisals, Revisions, Refutations.*

Chapter 9

Pathways to Reconciliation

The Israel-Palestine conflict is not only a struggle over land and resources but also a deeply emotional and psychological wound that has endured through generations. For a sustainable peace to take root, both communities must confront the traumas of the past, acknowledge injustices, and find a way to heal. A Truth and Reconciliation Commission (TRC) modeled after South Africa's post-apartheid process can play a pivotal role in helping both Israelis and Palestinians confront their painful histories, foster empathy, and create a foundation for forgiveness and healing.

The power of a TRC lies in its ability to create a space where individuals can share their experiences, recognize the humanity of the "other," and collectively mourn the losses sustained on both sides. Such a commission allows for the airing of grievances, an acknowledgment of suffering, and the opportunity to seek forgiveness—a vital step toward reconciliation. Archbishop Desmond Tutu's words capture the spirit of this process: "Forgiveness says you are given another chance to make a new beginning." Forgiveness is not about forgetting but about freeing oneself from the chains of the past, choosing instead to build a new future.

This chapter explores how a Truth and Reconciliation Commission could be structured within the Israel-Palestine confederation, the principles that would guide its work, and the potential outcomes of such a process. By addressing historical grievances and offering a platform for personal and communal healing, a TRC can help both communities move toward a new, unified identity rooted in mutual respect and understanding.

The Need for a Truth and Reconciliation Commission in Israel-Palestine

The longstanding nature of the Israel-Palestine conflict has created deep-seated bitterness, mistrust, and trauma. Many Israelis and Palestinians have experienced loss, violence, displacement, and discrimination, and these experiences shape each community's collective memory and identity. For Palestinians, the Nakba (the "catastrophe" of 1948) and subsequent occupation have left scars that fuel feelings of injustice and dispossession. For Israelis, years of hostility, terrorism, and fear of existential threat have reinforced the need for security and self-preservation.

These collective memories perpetuate division and make it difficult for either side to imagine a future together. Without an opportunity to address these traumas and seek mutual understanding, any peace achieved through political means risks being fragile and superficial. A Truth and Reconciliation Commission would provide a structured, systematic approach to healing, inviting both communities to participate in a shared journey toward peace and forgiveness.

Structuring the Truth and Reconciliation Commission

Creating an effective TRC for Israel and Palestine requires careful planning to ensure it is inclusive, impartial, and transparent. The commission would need to be structured in a way that allows for broad participation, balancing the voices of victims, perpetrators, and bystanders from both communities. This inclusivity ensures that the commission reflects the diversity of experiences within the region and promotes a sense of shared responsibility for healing.

Composition and Leadership

The commission would be composed of respected individuals from both Israeli and Palestinian communities, along with neutral international figures who can provide oversight and ensure impartiality. These individuals might include religious leaders, legal experts, psychologists, human rights advocates, and community organizers who have a reputation for fairness and a commitment to peace. Desmond Tutu's leadership of South Africa's TRC offers a powerful example of how religious and moral authority can lend credibility and compassion to the reconciliation process.

Leadership should be shared equally between Israeli and Palestinian representatives to symbolize the collaborative nature of this journey. Co-chairs—one Israeli and one Palestinian—would preside over the commission, supported by an international advisory panel that ensures fairness and transparency. This structure would help both communities feel equally represented, fostering trust in the commission's work.

Regional Committees and Accessibility

To reach as many people as possible, the TRC would establish regional committees in major cities and areas within both Israel and Palestine, including Jerusalem, Tel Aviv, Gaza, Ramallah, Haifa, and others. These committees would allow for localized hearings and smaller gatherings, where people can come together in accessible and familiar spaces. By decentralizing the TRC's operations, the commission can accommodate those who might feel uncomfortable or unsafe traveling to larger venues, thus encouraging broader participation.

Each regional committee would conduct hearings, gather testimonies, and facilitate dialogues. They would then report back to the central commission, which would compile findings and issue recommendations. By involving local communities, the TRC can foster grassroots involvement in the reconciliation process and ensure that all voices are heard.

Guiding Principles of the Truth and Reconciliation Commission

The TRC's success would depend on the principles that guide its work, ensuring that it remains focused on healing rather than blame. The commission should embody values of empathy, accountability, transparency, and respect for all participants, creating a space where healing can occur without fear of reprisal.

Truth-Seeking

One of the core principles of the TRC would be truth-seeking, providing a platform for individuals to share their experiences honestly and openly. Truth-seeking involves documenting the events and abuses that have occurred over the course of the conflict, including violence, displacement, and discrimination. By publicly acknowledging these events, the TRC offers validation to those who have suffered, helping them feel heard and recognized.

Truth-seeking is not only about individual experiences but also about constructing a shared historical narrative that both Israelis and Palestinians can acknowledge. Acknowledging past injustices is essential for creating a common foundation on which to build a future, as it allows both sides to move beyond denial or defensiveness and toward understanding.

Empathy and Compassion

The TRC would emphasize empathy and compassion, encouraging participants to listen to each other's stories with open hearts and minds. This principle is essential for breaking down stereotypes and humanizing those who have long been seen as "the other." Empathy fosters connections and understanding, helping Israelis and

Palestinians recognize their shared humanity and the pain that both communities have endured.

Commission facilitators would be trained in compassionate listening, and sessions would be structured to allow individuals to express their emotions without judgment. Testimonies might include stories of loss, survival, resilience, and even acts of kindness and solidarity across divides. By cultivating empathy, the TRC helps pave the way for forgiveness and reconciliation.

Accountability and Forgiveness

While the TRC would not have the power to prosecute individuals, it would emphasize accountability by providing a platform for individuals to take responsibility for their actions and express remorse. This principle does not seek to punish but to create an opportunity for individuals to seek forgiveness and for victims to find closure.

Forgiveness is a central tenet of the reconciliation process, yet it must be approached with sensitivity. As Desmond Tutu observed, "Forgiveness says you are given another chance to make a new beginning." Forgiveness cannot be imposed; it is a personal journey. However, the TRC can facilitate this journey by creating an environment where individuals feel safe to ask for forgiveness and to forgive, promoting healing without forcing it.

Potential Outcomes of the Truth and Reconciliation Commission

The potential outcomes of a TRC in Israel and Palestine extend beyond the individual healing of participants. A successful commission can help reshape collective memory, rebuild trust, and create the foundation for a unified, peaceful future.

Individual and Collective Healing

For many, participating in the TRC would be an opportunity to heal from trauma, release feelings of anger and bitterness, and find closure. Survivors of violence and displacement would have a platform to tell their stories, ensuring that their pain is acknowledged and validated. For those who have committed harm, the TRC provides a space to acknowledge their actions, seek forgiveness, and begin their own journey of reconciliation.

At a collective level, the TRC could help both communities move beyond narratives of victimization, allowing them to see each other not solely as victims or perpetrators but as human beings capable of change and redemption. By acknowledging each other's suffering, Israelis and Palestinians can begin to dismantle the stereotypes that perpetuate division and open the door to a shared identity based on empathy and respect.

Educational and Historical Records

The TRC's findings could be compiled into educational materials, books, documentaries, and exhibits that preserve the testimonies and narratives collected throughout the process. These resources would serve as an invaluable historical record, documenting the experiences of both Israelis and Palestinians for future generations. Schools could incorporate these materials into their curricula, helping young people understand the history of the conflict from multiple perspectives.

By preserving these testimonies, the TRC contributes to an enduring legacy of reconciliation. Future generations can learn from the past without carrying forward its wounds, building an informed and compassionate society.

Policy Recommendations and Institutional Reform

Based on its findings, the TRC could make policy recommendations to the Israel-Palestine confederation's government. These recommendations might include legal reforms to protect minority rights, policies to promote social cohesion, or reparations programs for communities that have experienced significant harm. For example, the TRC might propose reparations for displaced Palestinian families or suggest policies to protect both Palestinian and Jewish cultural heritage sites.

The TRC's recommendations would offer concrete steps for the government to address grievances, promote justice, and prevent future conflict. By addressing systemic issues through policy change, the TRC would help create a more equitable society, where peace is sustained by just and inclusive institutions.

The Role of International Support in the TRC

International support can play a vital role in ensuring the success and impartiality of the TRC. Countries with experience in truth and reconciliation processes, such as South Africa and Rwanda, could provide expertise, training, and resources. International observers could help maintain transparency, while NGOs and human rights organizations could offer resources for psychological support, mediation, and educational outreach.

International support could also help fund reparations and programs for victims, ensuring that the TRC's recommendations are implemented effectively. By involving the global community, the TRC can signal that the reconciliation process is an internationally recognized effort, encouraging accountability and solidarity with those seeking healing.

Conclusion: A New Beginning Through Reconciliation

A Truth and Reconciliation Commission is not a cure-all, but it is a powerful step toward healing the wounds of the past and building a foundation for a peaceful future. By providing a space for truth-telling, empathy, accountability, and forgiveness, the TRC can help Israelis and Palestinians transform their painful histories into shared lessons, fostering a spirit of reconciliation and renewal.

Desmond Tutu's words remind us that "Forgiveness says you are given another chance to make a new beginning." For Israelis and Palestinians, this chance at a new beginning represents hope—a hope that they can move forward not as adversaries bound by past grievances, but as neighbors committed to a shared, peaceful future. Through reconciliation, they can rewrite their collective story, building a society that values justice, compassion, and unity over division.

References

- **Tutu, D.** (1999). *No Future Without Forgiveness.*
- **Shlaim, A.** (2009). *Israel and Palestine: Reappraisals, Revisions, Refutations.*
- **Gobodo-Madikizela, P.** (2003). *A Human Being Died That Night: A South African Story of Forgiveness.*
- **Rothstein, R.** (2007). *After Apartheid: Reinventing South Africa?*

Chapter 10

Overcoming Challenges Together

The path to peace in Israel and Palestine is fraught with complex obstacles, many of which are deeply rooted in the historical, psychological, and social fabric of both communities. Achieving a sustainable and just peace through the confederation model will require resilience, adaptability, and a profound commitment to patience and empathy. The challenges are significant: from political resistance by hardliners on both sides to logistical difficulties in implementing cooperative governance structures. Yet, it is precisely through addressing these obstacles together, step-by-step, that the confederation can build a future where mutual understanding, respect, and interdependence are possible.

As theologian Stanley Hauerwas reminds us, "The hard task of peace is that it requires patience—patience with ourselves and patience with those we would hope to be our friends." Patience is the cornerstone of building trust, healing wounds, and fostering the confidence needed to overcome obstacles that have derailed peace efforts in the past. This chapter delves into the anticipated challenges facing the confederation, strategies for phased implementation, and the importance of confidence-building measures to ensure lasting success.

Identifying Key Obstacles to Peace

While the confederation model holds great promise, it also faces considerable opposition and logistical challenges. By identifying and understanding these obstacles, the confederation can craft thoughtful, adaptive responses to address them effectively.

Political Resistance from Hardliners

One of the most prominent challenges in implementing a confederation is resistance from hardliners on both sides. These groups—ranging from political parties to social organizations and influential individuals—often hold rigid views regarding territorial sovereignty and security. In Israel, nationalist factions may view any collaboration with Palestinians as a compromise on security or a relinquishment of land. Similarly, in Palestine, factions that have endured years of occupation and inequality may see cooperation as capitulation rather than empowerment.

Addressing hardline resistance requires recognizing the fears and insecurities that underpin these views. Many hardliners fear that compromise may erode their cultural or religious identity or lead to perceived losses in security and autonomy. To overcome these fears, the confederation will need to offer tangible guarantees, transparency, and a vision of mutual benefit that reassures hardliners that peace will not come at the expense of their core values or security.

Distrust and Historical Grievances

Decades of violence, trauma, and displacement have created a deep well of distrust between Israelis and Palestinians. Both communities carry historical grievances that are passed down through generations, fostering narratives of victimhood and blame. This distrust is not easily overcome and is reinforced by each new conflict or perceived slight. For some, the idea of a shared government and legal system is inconceivable without first addressing these deeply ingrained wounds.

Building trust requires long-term commitment and sustained efforts to engage with both communities at every level. Reconciliation efforts, such as the Truth and Reconciliation Commission discussed in Chapter 9, will be crucial in addressing historical grievances, while confidence-building measures can create a foundation of trust on which the confederation can be constructed.

Socioeconomic Disparities

Socioeconomic disparities between Israelis and Palestinians, particularly in employment, healthcare, infrastructure, and education, pose another challenge to the success of the confederation. Disparities can breed resentment and feelings of injustice, undermining efforts to build a unified, cooperative society. Addressing these inequalities will require a comprehensive approach that promotes economic justice, shared opportunities, and equitable access to resources.

By implementing revenue-sharing mechanisms, joint infrastructure projects, and educational and economic initiatives, the confederation can work to reduce these disparities over time. However, achieving socioeconomic equality is a long-term project, one that requires commitment, investment, and the resilience to face setbacks along the way.

Security Concerns

Security is a significant concern for both communities, and fears surrounding potential security threats can hinder cooperation. Israelis and Palestinians alike have experienced violence and terrorism, creating a pervasive sense of vulnerability. Without assurances that their security needs will be addressed, many may be reluctant to support a confederation.

A unified security approach, as described in Chapter 6, can help alleviate these concerns by fostering a cooperative security system that prioritizes the safety of all residents. Additionally, ongoing communication, transparency, and collaboration in security matters will help reassure both communities that their safety is being managed effectively within the framework of the confederation.

Phased Implementation: A Step-by-Step Approach to Building Peace

Given the depth and complexity of these challenges, the confederation must adopt a phased implementation strategy that allows both Israelis and Palestinians to gradually adapt to new structures and build trust incrementally. Phased implementation involves dividing the process of building a confederation into manageable stages, with each stage focusing on specific goals, testing the efficacy of initiatives, and building confidence over time.

Phase 1: Building Initial Trust and Confidence

The first phase of implementation would focus on establishing trust and creating visible symbols of cooperation. Initial steps could include:

Confidence-Building Measures: Launch joint projects that demonstrate the benefits of cooperation without requiring immediate political concessions. These might include joint infrastructure initiatives, environmental conservation projects, or public health campaigns that benefit both communities. Visible, positive outcomes from these projects can help build confidence in the confederation model.

Educational and Cultural Exchange Programs: Organizing cross-community educational programs, cultural exchanges, and dialogues can promote understanding and humanize each community in the eyes of the other. Schools could implement curricula that explore shared histories and cultural heritages, helping young people see their neighbors in a new light.

Establishment of Joint Councils for Specific Issues: Form initial joint councils focused on specific, practical issues, such as water resource management or environmental protection. These councils would allow both sides to practice collaborative governance in a low-stakes environment, developing trust and learning how to work together effectively.

Phase 2: Strengthening Joint Institutions

Once initial trust has been established, the second phase would focus on expanding joint governance structures and creating institutions that address shared concerns. This phase could include:

Establishing a Joint Legal Framework: Begin implementing the joint legal framework discussed in Chapter 8, with initial pilot courts that handle cross-border disputes and inter-community cases. These courts would serve as a testbed for broader legal cooperation, allowing both communities to experience the benefits of impartial, shared justice mechanisms.

Cooperative Security Programs: Launch cooperative security programs with mixed patrols and joint training initiatives, as outlined in Chapter 6. These programs would provide practical experience in shared security operations and demonstrate that a unified approach can ensure safety for all.

Revenue Sharing and Economic Integration: Implement revenue-sharing mechanisms to address economic disparities, beginning with joint infrastructure projects and shared public services. Gradually expanding economic integration, especially in high-impact sectors like agriculture and tourism, can help both communities see tangible benefits from the confederation.

Phase 3: Full Implementation and Institutional Consolidation

In the third phase, the confederation would move toward full implementation, consolidating institutions and expanding governance structures. At this stage:

Complete Integration of Joint Courts and Legal Protections: Fully implement the joint legal system, ensuring that it is accessible to all citizens, with robust protections for minority rights and representation. By this phase, both communities should have a strong understanding and trust in the shared legal framework.

Establishing a Central Governing Body: The confederation's central governing body would assume full authority over shared issues, including trade, immigration, and environmental regulation. This governing body would represent both communities equitably and address ongoing needs and challenges through consensus-driven decision-making.

Public Celebration and Cultural Events: Organize public events and ceremonies celebrating the achievements of the confederation, involving leaders from both communities. These events reinforce the sense of shared identity and accomplishment, helping cement the confederation as a long-term partnership.

Confidence-Building Measures: The Key to Sustained Progress

To overcome challenges, confidence-building measures (CBMs) must be woven into every phase of the implementation process. These CBMs are designed to foster trust, demonstrate goodwill, and create a positive atmosphere for cooperation. Successful CBMs should be visible, inclusive, and emphasize shared values and goals.

Transparency and Open Communication

Transparency in all aspects of the confederation is essential to overcoming distrust. Regular updates, open communication from leaders, and accessible reports on the progress of the confederation's initiatives can reassure both communities that they are equal partners in this endeavor. This transparency helps prevent misunderstandings, rumors, and suspicions from undermining progress.

Media and Public Awareness Campaigns

Media plays a powerful role in shaping public perception. Positive media coverage of the confederation's achievements, joint initiatives, and success stories can help build support for peace. The confederation could partner with journalists, filmmakers, and influencers from both communities to create content that highlights the benefits of cooperation, humanizes both sides, and promotes a vision of shared prosperity.

Community-Based Dialogue Initiatives

Involving local communities in dialogue and reconciliation initiatives can build support from the grassroots level. Community leaders, religious figures, educators, and youth organizations can facilitate open discussions about the confederation, allowing individuals to express concerns and ask questions. By addressing fears and misconceptions directly, community-based dialogues can foster a sense of agency and investment in the success of the confederation.

The Importance of Patience and Perseverance

The journey toward a peaceful and prosperous confederation will not be easy or swift. Setbacks, challenges, and moments of tension are inevitable, and the process will require patience and perseverance from both communities. Stanley Hauerwas reminds us that "The hard task of peace is that it requires patience—patience with ourselves and patience with those we would hope to be our friends." This patience is not passive; it is an active commitment to continue working together, even when difficulties arise.

Patience requires leaders who can maintain a long-term perspective, recognizing that peace is a process that unfolds over years and even generations. It demands humility, a willingness to listen, and the courage to forgive. Through patience, both communities can gradually overcome the challenges they face, moving closer to the vision of a united, peaceful confederation.

Conclusion: Together, Toward a Future of Shared Peace

Overcoming challenges together is not just a necessity—it is an opportunity. The obstacles that stand in the way of peace are also the very mechanisms through which Israelis and Palestinians can forge a stronger, more resilient partnership. By addressing political resistance, mistrust, socioeconomic disparities, and security concerns, the confederation can demonstrate that cooperation is not only possible but essential.

Through phased implementation, confidence-building measures, and a steadfast commitment to patience, the confederation can gradually transform from a political arrangement into a lived reality. Together, Israelis and Palestinians can move toward a future where peace is not only a possibility but a shared journey. The hard work of overcoming these challenges can lay the groundwork for a society that honors both its diversity and its unity, offering future generations a foundation of hope, justice, and mutual respect.

References

Hauerwas, S. (1981). *A Community of Character: Toward a Constructive Christian Social Ethic.*

- **Kriesberg, L.** (1998). *Constructive Conflicts: From Escalation to Resolution.*
- **Kelman, H. C.** (1999). *Transforming the Israeli-Palestinian Conflict: From Mutual Negation to Reconciliation.*

Chapter 11

International Support and Oversight

For the Israel-Palestine confederation to thrive, it requires a framework of international support and oversight that ensures fairness, accountability, and stability. While a successful confederation depends on the commitment and cooperation of Israelis and Palestinians, neutral international actors such as the United Nations (UN), the European Union (EU), and other global organizations can play an instrumental role in providing support and mediation, offering resources, and maintaining a structure of impartial oversight. This international presence would be designed to empower and stabilize the confederation without imposing external control, ensuring that the peace process remains owned by the people it seeks to unite.

Reinhold Niebuhr's words, "Man's capacity for justice makes democracy possible; but man's inclination to injustice makes democracy necessary," are a timely reminder that while we can aspire to fairness and peace, mechanisms must be in place to safeguard these ideals against potential injustice. International law and oversight can serve as these mechanisms, providing a check against the inclinations toward power imbalance, mistrust, or the resurgence of old grievances. In this chapter, we examine the roles of international law and oversight, explore potential contributions from global institutions, and propose ways in which these actors can support a balanced, just, and transparent confederation in Israel-Palestine.

The Role of International Law in Supporting Justice and Accountability

International law provides a foundation upon which peace agreements and cooperative frameworks can be built. By integrating international legal standards and human rights principles into the confederation's governing documents, the Israel-Palestine confederation can ensure that its policies reflect universal principles of justice, equality, and human rights. This integration would reinforce the confederation's commitment to upholding the dignity of all individuals, regardless of nationality, religion, or ethnicity.

Adopting International Human Rights Standards

A key aspect of international support is the incorporation of human rights protections within the confederation's constitution or governing charter. These protections could be based on established documents like the Universal Declaration of Human Rights, the Geneva Conventions, and other human rights treaties that both Israel and Palestine have ratified. By embedding these protections, the confederation would commit to safeguarding civil liberties, minority rights, and fundamental freedoms, which are essential for a peaceful coexistence.

An independent human rights commission, potentially supported by international experts, could monitor adherence to these standards, investigate alleged violations, and recommend corrective actions. This commission would report its findings to both the confederation's central government and to international bodies, ensuring transparency and accountability.

Supporting a Fair and Equitable Legal System

International legal experts, including judges and lawyers with experience in conflict resolution and transitional justice, can assist the confederation in establishing a fair and impartial legal system. Their expertise would be particularly valuable in setting up joint courts, arbitration mechanisms, and minority rights protections, as discussed in Chapter 8. The international community can also provide training for local legal professionals to ensure that the joint legal system reflects best practices and operates independently of political pressure.

Neutral international bodies, such as the International Court of Justice or the International Criminal Court, could serve as a venue of last resort for unresolved or serious disputes. This external option would create an additional layer of accountability, ensuring that even the highest levels of power within the confederation remain subject to impartial oversight.

Roles and Contributions of Key International Actors

Various international organizations and countries could play different roles in supporting the confederation, from providing financial resources and technical expertise to acting as mediators in times of tension. Each actor would contribute in a way that respects the autonomy of the confederation while supporting its goals of peace, justice, and prosperity.

United Nations (UN)

The UN has extensive experience in peacekeeping, conflict resolution, and post-conflict reconstruction, making it well-suited to provide support to the Israel-Palestine confederation. A UN mission could be established to monitor security, assist with mediation efforts, and oversee humanitarian aid distribution. This mission would not involve military forces but rather rely on civilian experts in governance, human rights, and community-building. The UN's presence would signal the international community's commitment to supporting the confederation without imposing an external agenda.

The UN could also facilitate regular reviews of the confederation's progress toward peace, organizing biannual or annual forums where representatives from Israel, Palestine, and relevant international actors come together to assess the situation and make adjustments to their approach. These reviews would ensure accountability and provide a forum for dialogue and reflection.

European Union (EU)

The EU's role as a political and economic union offers a valuable model for how diverse states can cooperate across borders. The EU could provide technical expertise and financial assistance to support infrastructure projects, economic development, and educational initiatives within the confederation. The EU's experience in building institutions that promote cross-border trade, open movement, and cultural exchange could guide similar efforts in Israel-Palestine.

Additionally, the EU's diplomatic influence can help mediate disputes and encourage political support for the confederation among neighboring countries. By acting as a bridge between Israel, Palestine, and other Middle Eastern states, the EU could foster regional cooperation, further stabilizing the confederation and enhancing its economic potential.

International Financial Institutions

Institutions like the World Bank, the International Monetary Fund (IMF), and regional development banks can provide essential financial support for the confederation's development needs. With significant economic disparities existing between Israel and Palestine, funding for infrastructure, healthcare, education, and job creation will be necessary to create a balanced and equitable economy. Grants, low-interest loans, and technical assistance from these institutions could help finance joint projects, reduce poverty, and promote sustainable development.

These financial institutions could also support the confederation in establishing a transparent budgeting process, fostering economic interdependence and accountability. With international support, the confederation can create revenue-sharing mechanisms, as discussed in Chapter 7, that distribute resources fairly and reduce economic inequalities.

Role of Neighboring Countries

Neighboring countries, particularly Egypt, Jordan, and other members of the Arab League, can play a critical role in supporting the confederation by promoting regional stability, facilitating cross-border trade, and endorsing the confederation as a legitimate and positive step toward peace. Diplomatic and economic partnerships with neighboring states can offer the confederation additional pathways for economic growth and integration into the broader Middle East.

Neighboring countries can also offer support in areas of cultural and educational exchange, helping the confederation's citizens build ties across the region. This regional acceptance is essential for ensuring that the confederation feels secure within the Middle Eastern context and that Israelis and Palestinians can see themselves as part of a broader, supportive network of nations.

Ensuring Accountability and Transparency through Oversight Mechanisms

International oversight mechanisms are essential to uphold the confederation's commitment to justice, transparency, and accountability. These mechanisms would support the confederation's governance structures, ensure compliance with agreements, and offer a recourse for grievances, thus helping both communities feel secure in the new political arrangement.

Establishing an Independent Oversight Body

An independent oversight body composed of respected international legal, political, and human rights experts could monitor the confederation's governance and provide impartial evaluations of its progress. This body would report directly to the UN, EU, and other supporting institutions, issuing annual reports that evaluate adherence to human rights, the rule of law, and democratic principles. The oversight body would also serve as a mediator for disputes, providing recommendations for resolving conflicts that arise within the confederation.

Regular Monitoring and Reporting

To maintain accountability, the oversight body would conduct regular monitoring of political, economic, and social conditions within the confederation. This monitoring would include site visits, interviews with citizens, and assessments of key institutions. Reports could cover issues such as adherence to minority rights protections, the functioning of joint institutions, and the effectiveness of revenue-sharing mechanisms.

By publishing these reports publicly, the oversight body would promote transparency and give both communities insight into the strengths and weaknesses of the confederation. Public access to these reports would empower citizens, enabling them to hold their leaders accountable and engage in meaningful discussions about the confederation's future.

Safeguarding Minority Rights

One of the oversight body's critical functions would be to monitor and protect the rights of minorities within the confederation. With both

Israelis and Palestinians representing significant populations in each other's regions, the protection of minority rights is vital to maintaining harmony and fostering a sense of belonging. The oversight body could investigate reports of discrimination, monitor the implementation of language and cultural rights, and recommend policy changes to protect minority communities.

In cases of alleged rights violations, the oversight body could collaborate with the confederation's human rights commission to investigate, mediate, and provide recommendations for corrective actions. By actively safeguarding minority rights, international oversight can help both communities feel secure and valued within the confederation.

Confidence-Building Through International Partnerships and Diplomacy

International partnerships and diplomatic efforts can play an essential role in building confidence within the confederation, reassuring both Israelis and Palestinians that they have the support of a global community invested in their success.

Cultural Exchange Programs

International cultural exchange programs involving Israelis, Palestinians, and individuals from various countries could promote mutual understanding and highlight the benefits of diversity within the confederation. Exchanges with other multicultural societies, such as those within the EU or Africa, could help Israelis and Palestinians learn from the experiences of others who have navigated complex cultural and political landscapes. These programs, funded and facilitated by international partners, would emphasize the values of tolerance, collaboration, and shared identity.

Diplomatic Recognition and Trade Agreements

Support from the international community through diplomatic recognition and trade agreements can further legitimize the confederation and boost its economic potential. Bilateral and multilateral trade agreements with countries around the world could provide new markets for Israeli and Palestinian goods, encouraging economic growth and job creation. Diplomatic recognition, particularly from influential global powers, would strengthen the confederation's standing on the world stage, demonstrating that the peace process is a legitimate and valued part of the international community.

Conclusion: Building a Secure, Just, and Transparent Future with International Support

The role of international support and oversight in the Israel-Palestine confederation is not to control or dictate the path to peace but to create a supportive framework that enables both communities to thrive. Neutral international actors provide the tools, resources, and accountability necessary to foster justice, equality, and transparency within the confederation. Through international law, financial support, diplomatic partnerships, and oversight mechanisms, the global community can help Israelis and Palestinians build a future rooted in mutual respect and shared prosperity.

Reinhold Niebuhr's words serve as a powerful reminder that peace and justice require not only good intentions but also checks and balances to prevent injustice and protect the rights of all individuals. The confederation's success depends on its commitment to these principles, with the international community standing as a trusted partner in the pursuit of a sustainable peace. With the support of the global community, the Israel-Palestine confederation has the opportunity to serve as a model for cooperative governance, resilience, and the power of shared responsibility.

References

- **Niebuhr, R.** (1932). *Moral Man and Immoral Society.*
- **Baker, R. W.** (1990). *International Law and the Middle East Conflict: Towards an Informed Framework for Peace.*
- **Smith, C. D.** (2013). *Palestine and the Arab-Israeli Conflict.*
- **Lapidoth, R.** (1992). *The United Nations and the Palestinian Question: Reappraisal.*

Chapter 12

Conclusion: A Shared Future

The journey toward a peaceful Israel-Palestine confederation is more than a political endeavor; it is a profound transformation that demands reimagining coexistence at every level. For too long, the Israel-Palestine conflict has been framed as a zero-sum game, where gains for one community are seen as losses for the other. This vision of peace transcends that narrative, asserting that true peace is not merely the absence of war or the signing of treaties but a continuous, daily practice of respect, dignity, and humility. It is a peace that must be cultivated in the shared spaces, institutions, and interactions of everyday life, where individuals from both communities recognize their mutual responsibility to build a just, compassionate society.

Throughout this book, we have explored the complex and multifaceted steps needed to achieve this vision of a shared future. Each chapter has illuminated different aspects of this journey—from security cooperation and economic integration to legal protections and international support. Together, these elements form a framework that can foster genuine reconciliation and sustainable peace. As Stanley Hauerwas writes in *War and the American Difference*, "Peace is a hard task, requiring patience and humility." The final chapter reinforces that this shared future is possible only through humility and a commitment to the values that honor both God and humanity. "When bombs and muscles fail," Hauerwas suggests, "humility is the majesty that honors God and humanity." This closing reflection on humility, compassion, and courage speaks to the deep-rooted change required to embrace each other's humanity, heal the wounds of history, and build a future defined not by division but by shared hope and purpose.

A Vision of Shared Responsibility

The concept of shared responsibility is at the heart of the confederation model. This approach challenges both Israelis and Palestinians to see beyond historical grievances, mistrust, and fear, and to recognize that their fates are intertwined. The confederation is not merely a political arrangement; it is a call to participate in each other's lives, to listen, to empathize, and to commit to a future where both communities have equal opportunities and security.

This responsibility extends to each aspect of the confederation—whether it's joint security forces patrolling shared borders, economic partnerships creating jobs and growth, or a legal system that upholds justice for all citizens. Every interaction, every decision, becomes an opportunity to practice coexistence. Through this shared responsibility, Israelis and Palestinians can begin to see each other not as threats or competitors but as partners in a common endeavor, bound by the shared task of peace.

Humility and Compassion as the Foundation of True Peace

In a region scarred by conflict, the virtue of humility is often overshadowed by the pursuit of power, control, and dominance. However, as Hauerwas eloquently reminds us, true peace requires humility—a recognition that no one community possesses all the answers or holds exclusive claims to justice. Humility is the courage to accept one's limitations, to seek understanding, and to extend compassion even in moments of vulnerability.

Humility allows Israelis and Palestinians to move beyond a mindset of "winning" or "losing" and instead to view each other as equals in the pursuit of a shared future. It encourages individuals to listen without judgment, to ask for forgiveness, and to forgive in return. In extending compassion, Israelis and Palestinians honor the intrinsic dignity of each person, reflecting the spiritual and ethical values that underpin Judaism, Islam, and Christianity alike. This compassion becomes the bridge that can transform strangers into neighbors and adversaries into friends.

The Practice of Daily Coexistence

Peace is not achieved in grand gestures alone; it is sustained in the quiet, daily interactions that build trust and understanding. The vision for the confederation emphasizes practical steps toward coexistence—joint institutions, open borders, shared economic opportunities—that bring Israelis and Palestinians into contact and collaboration on a regular basis. Whether it's working together in a joint council, attending schools that emphasize multicultural understanding, or participating in neighborhood exchanges, these daily encounters humanize each community in the eyes of the other, fostering the empathy and solidarity needed to sustain peace.

This practice of daily coexistence requires patience. As both communities learn to navigate shared spaces, they will encounter challenges, misunderstandings, and setbacks. But through these experiences, they will also gain resilience and the capacity to see each other as allies in a shared journey. Over time, coexistence will no longer be seen as a necessity imposed by political compromise but as a natural and enriching part of life.

Embracing Humanity: The Courage to Heal

The Israel-Palestine conflict has inflicted deep emotional and psychological scars on both sides, and healing from these wounds demands courage. The courage to heal is not about forgetting the past but about choosing to move forward together despite it. Embracing humanity means acknowledging the pain and suffering that each community has endured while choosing not to be defined by it. It means choosing hope over bitterness, reconciliation over retribution.

A Truth and Reconciliation Commission, as discussed in Chapter 9, can provide an essential platform for this healing process. By allowing individuals to share their experiences, confront painful truths, and seek forgiveness, Israelis and Palestinians can release the burdens of the past and create space for healing and reconciliation. This courage to heal, to listen, and to forgive is what will ultimately allow both communities to transcend the cycle of fear and retribution and embrace a new, shared identity based on mutual respect.

International Support as a Bridge, Not a Crutch

Throughout this book, we have underscored the role of international support in facilitating peace, justice, and accountability. The presence of neutral international actors, whether through diplomatic support, legal oversight, or economic assistance, provides the stability and security needed to ensure that the confederation can flourish.

However, this international support should be seen as a bridge to peace, not a crutch upon which the confederation depends indefinitely.

The ultimate goal is for Israelis and Palestinians to take full ownership of the confederation and to build a self-sustaining system that no longer relies on external intervention. International support can offer guidance, resources, and encouragement, but the real work of peace must be carried out by the people of Israel and Palestine themselves. It is only through their active participation, commitment, and dedication that this vision of a shared future can endure.

The Promise of a New Generation

The hope for a peaceful Israel-Palestine confederation rests in the hands of future generations. For many young Israelis and Palestinians, the conflict is all they have ever known. Yet, they are also the most open to new ideas, less burdened by the scars of past battles, and eager to create a better world. Through educational initiatives, cultural exchanges, and youth leadership programs, the confederation can empower a new generation to break free from the patterns of division and embrace a vision of unity.

Young people can be the bridge-builders, the innovators, and the peacemakers who carry forward the legacy of peace with a fresh perspective. By fostering youth engagement, the confederation can instill in young Israelis and Palestinians the values of empathy, cooperation, and shared responsibility, equipping them to lead their communities into a future defined not by conflict but by collaboration.

A Lasting Legacy of Peace

The Israel-Palestine confederation represents more than a solution to a political conflict; it is a testament to the transformative power of reconciliation, humility, and shared responsibility. By choosing to build a future together, Israelis and Palestinians honor not only each other but also the broader ideals of justice, compassion, and peace. This confederation can serve as a model for other regions facing intractable conflicts, demonstrating that even the most entrenched divisions can be bridged through patience, empathy, and a commitment to the common good.

As this book concludes, it is important to remember that peace is a journey, not a destination. The path to a shared future will be filled with challenges, uncertainties, and sacrifices. But through humility, courage, and an unwavering commitment to justice, both communities can transform this vision into reality.

The Final Call: "When Bombs and Muscles Fail, Humility is the Majesty That Honors God and Humanity."

This closing statement encapsulates the essence of the Israel-Palestine confederation. Peace is not achieved through force, dominance, or fear; it is found in the quiet strength of humility, compassion, and a willingness to see the divine in each other. True peace is built on the courage to extend a hand, to recognize shared humanity, and to honor the dignity of every person. In choosing this path, Israelis and Palestinians create a legacy that honors their history, their faiths, and their shared home.

The Israel-Palestine confederation offers a new beginning—a chance to make peace a lived reality rather than an elusive dream. This future belongs not only to Israelis and Palestinians but to humanity as a whole, as a testament to the power of humility and the enduring hope for a world defined by justice, compassion, and unity.

References

- **Hauerwas, S.** (2010). *War and the American Difference: Theological Reflections on Violence and National Identity.*
- **Gopin, M.** (2000). *Between Eden and Armageddon: The Future of World*

Religions, Violence, and Peacemaking.

- **Khalidi, R.** (2020). *The Hundred Years' War on Palestine.*
- **Abu-Nimer, M.** (2003). *Nonviolence and Peace Building in Islam: Theory and Practice.*

Don't miss out!

Visit the website below and you can sign up to receive emails whenever Kayumba David publishes a new book. There's no charge and no obligation.

https://books2read.com/r/B-A-KRSOC-KREGF

BOOKS 2 READ

Connecting independent readers to independent writers.

Did you love *Bridging the Rift: A Pacifist Vision for the Israel-Palestine Future*? Then you should read *Hope and Healing: A Chaplain's Handbook*[1] by Kayumba David!

[2]

As a survivor of a challenging illness, I have experienced firsthand the profound impact that compassionate care can have on individuals in their most vulnerable moments. My journey through a robust healthcare environment in Belgium illuminated the critical role that various professionals play in the healing process. Nurses, doctors, and countless other healthcare staff dedicate themselves to the well-being of their patients, often going above and beyond to ensure that each person feels valued and cared for. Their unwavering commitment to service inspires not only hope but also a sense of dignity during difficult times.

---

1. https://books2read.com/u/mg6dYX

2. https://books2read.com/u/mg6dYX

In writing this book, I am compelled to reflect on the significant contributions of those who serve in hospitals and other care settings, particularly chaplains who offer spiritual guidance and emotional support. They are the quiet yet powerful voices that provide comfort, instilling hope where despair often threatens to take root. Chaplains walk alongside patients and families, navigating the challenges of illness, suffering, and the uncertainty of life and death.

This guide aims to illuminate the path of chaplaincy in various environments, particularly within hospitals and prisons. It is a call to those who feel the tug of a sacred vocation, encouraging them to embrace their role as vessels of God's love and grace. It is my hope that this book serves as a source of inspiration and practical guidance for current and future chaplains, empowering them to foster healing, reconciliation, and transformation in the lives of those they serve.

May this work resonate with anyone who seeks to understand the beauty and importance of compassionate ministry, reminding us all of the profound difference that care and hope can make in our world.

Read more at www.zcews.org.

About the Author

Kayumba David is an accomplished author known for his works that span across themes of spirituality, African experiences, and healthcare chaplaincy. His writings often delve into profound social, political, and personal subjects.

One of his notable works is "Visas: The Irony of Freedom", where he critiques the paradoxes faced by many Africans regarding international travel and freedom

He also authored "Hope and Healing: A Chaplain's Handbook," which reflects on his experiences as a chaplain and emphasizes the importance of compassion and spiritual care in healthcare and prison environments

Kayumba's works reflect his personal journey through theological study and lay ministry, having faced challenges within religious institutions, especially during his time in Belgium, where he became an advocate for open theological debate

His contributions in literature offer insights into African realities, the complexities of modern spirituality, and the role of chaplaincy in emotional healing.

Read more at www.zcews.org.